TYPO3 4.3 Multimedia Cookbook

Over 50 great recipes for effectively managing multimedia content to create an organized website in TYPO3

Dan Osipov

BIRMINGHAM - MUMBAI

TYPO3 4.3 Multimedia Cookbook

Copyright © 2010 Packt Publishing

First published: January 2010

Production Reference: 1210110

Published by Packt Publishing Ltd.
32 Lincoln Road
Olton
Birmingham, B27 6PA, UK.

ISBN 978-1-847198-48-8

www.packtpub.com

Cover Image by Vinayak Chittar (vinayak.chittar@gmail.com)

Credits

Author
Dan Osipov

Reviewers
Karsten Dambekalns

Mario Rimann

Mathias Schreiber

Acquisition Editor
Rashmi Phadnis

Development Editor
Reshma Sundaresan

Technical Editor
Kavita Iyer

Copy Editor
Ajay Shanker

Indexer
Hemangini Bari

Editorial Team Leader
Mithun Sehgal

Project Team Leader
Lata Basantani

Project Coordinator
Poorvi Nair

Proofreader
Andie Scothern

Graphics
Nilesh R. Mohite

Production Coordinator
Adline Swetha Jesuthas

Cover Work
Adline Swetha Jesuthas

About the Author

Dan Osipov has over 12 years of web development, graphic design, as well as system architecture and application development experience. He has worked on various multipurpose sites, including e-commerce, educational, informational, and dynamic news sites. For the last 4 years, he has worked in the media industry, designing and maintaining an online presence for journals and newspapers.

At the moment of writing, Dan was employed at Calkins Media, where he worked on using TYPO3 as the CMS system powering high traffic, dynamic news sites, like phillyBrubs. com and Timesonline.com. He is also a member of the Digital Asset Management team, focused on the development of the DAM extension for TYPO3.

I would like to thank the Phillyburbs team, as their needs served as an inspiration for a lot of the material in this book. I would like to thank the TYPO3 community at large for "inspiring people to share". Last, but not least, I would like to thank my family for their understanding and support.

About the Reviewers

Karsten Dambekalns, born in 1977, learned the basics of web technology the hard way – by looking at other websites' HTML source. This happened after having learned BASIC and Assembler on a good old Commodore C128.

Karsten discovered PHP in 1999 and and was caught by TYPO3's immense possibilities in 2002. Later, he joined the TYPO3 Association and today is part of the TYPO3 5.0 and FLOW3 development team.

In 2000, he founded his own Internet company together with a friend from university, which he left behind in 2008 to become a freelancer working fully on the development of TYPO3. Karsten also speaks at conferences and writes articles about topics around PHP and TYPO3.

Karsten mostly lives in Germany with his wife Līga, their three kids, and a nameless Espresso machine.

Mario Rimann, born in 1982 in Zürich, Switzerland, started his journey through the IT jungle back in the early 90s. After his primary education as a service technician for office equipment like printers, copy machines, fax machines, and computers, he moved to his first job as a system administrator at a school. After collecting some years of IT and "people-skills", Mario moved onto the European headquarters of a company running a big website in the nightlife business, later he had his own company, and is now again a regular employee.

While being employed at the above-mentioned school, he made his first contact with TYPO3. In the beginning, it was mainly a hobby—which evolved to be the main part of his own company. In 2006 and 2007, he organized the first two international TYPO3 Developer Days, which took place in Switzerland.

Right now, Mario is employed as a project manager and developer at a mid-sized web-agency in central Switzerland that specializes in TYPO3 and Magento.

Alongside his job, Mario also helps out in several TYPO3 projects.

You can contact him at mario@rimann.org.

Mathias Schreiber has been working in the Web industry since 1995, developing websites with database-driven content for several large companies throughout Europe. He has been a part of the TYPO3 community since early 2002. Ever since then, he has been close to the core development and also hosted early developer meetings in 2004.

He did more than 100 training sessions in Germany and Switzerland spreading the word about TYPO3 and has trained most of today's successful TYPO3 companies.

In 2004, he founded wmdb Systems together with Peter Kühn, Diana Beer, and Bodo Eichstaedt and since then he maintains large TYPO3 projects for many well-known companies from Europe.

For two years, he has been part of the 12 so called active members of the TYPO3 Association but resigned from his duties to focus on his company and family.

Today, you can find him on almost any TYPO3 event there is—training snowboard-beginners at the TYPO3 Snowboard tours, mentoring bug-fixing sessions on the TYPO3 Developer days, or sharing ideas on the TYPO3 Conference.

Table of Contents

Preface

TYPO3 is one of the world's leading open source content management systems, written in PHP, which can be used to create and customize your website. Along with text content, you can display high quality images, audio, and video to your site's visitors by using TYPO3. It is essential to manage various types of multimedia files in content management systems for both editors and the users on the frontend of the site.

This book gives you the step-by-step process for organizing an effective multimedia system. It also gives solutions to commonly encountered problems, and offers a variety of tools for dealing with multimedia content. The author's experience in large-scale systems enables him to share his effective solutions to these problems.

What this book covers

Chapter 1, *Getting Started* introduces the reader to TYPO3, and helps set up a basic website; where the material in this chapter alone is not enough, the user is directed to other resources to fill in the gaps of knowledge in order to proceed further.

Chapter 2, *Managing Digital Assets* introduces the reader to the concept of digital asset management. Accounts for various groups of users (editors, administrators, web users) are created and assigned permissions. We also create a first extension that allows web users to upload files into the system.

Chapter 3, *Operating with Metadata in Media Files* expands upon the digital asset management idea, and cover file metadata, which can be used to classify files. The chapter covers various types and formats of metadata, and how it can be extracted in TYPO3.

Chapter 4, *Rendering Images* covers how images can be included on a TYPO3-driven website using content elements and a TYPO3 script. It also covers how to embed images in Rich Text Editor. You will learn to render links to media files, create a gallery, and render metadata using a DAM object.

Chapter 5, *Rendering Video and Audio* explains how you will render audio and video using media content object, TypoScript Object, content elements, and rgmediaimages extension. You will play video using a custom media player and Flash Media Server. We will also create new plugins for rendering audio files.

Chapter 6, *Connecting to External APIs* shows how external services, specifically Amazon S3, Flickr, and YouTube, can be leveraged to expand the system. We pull in files from YouTube and Flickr. We also use Amazon S3 to provide us with limitless storage.

Chapter 7, *Creating Services* covers services and hooks—powerful concepts in TYPO3, which allow individual sites to add different processing capabilities depending on the system. We use services to parse metadata, and convert files.

Chapter 8, *Automating Processes* describes how some processes and workflows could be automated; making the computer do all the hard work, while the editor oversees the process.

What you need for this book

In order to get the most from this book, there are some expectations of prior knowledge and experience. It is assumed that the reader has a good understanding of TYPO3, which can be achieved by reading the introductory tutorials—*Inside TYPO3*, *TYPO3 Core API*, and *Modern Template Building guide*—essential to understand how TYPO3 works. Basic TypoScript knowledge is required as well.

Who this book is for

This book is for anyone who is looking for effective systems for managing and operating with multimedia content. You will find this book interesting if you are running, or starting websites rich in multimedia content.

This book assumes some prior knowledge of TYPO3, which is available either from the official documentation, or other books on this topic.

Conventions

In this book, you will find a number of styles of text that distinguish between different kinds of information. Here are some examples of these styles, and an explanation of their meaning.

Code words in text are shown as follows: "We can include other contexts through the use of the `include` directive."

A block of code is set as follows:

```
<IfModule mod_fcgid.c>
  AddHandler fcgid-script .fcgi
  SocketPath /var/lib/apache2/fcgid/sock
```

```
    IPCConnectTimeout 60
    IPCCommTimeout 256
    BusyTimeout 256
    ProcessLifeTime 256
</IfModule>
```

When we wish to draw your attention to a particular part of a code block, the relevant lines or items are set in bold:

```
class tx_myext_ftpDownload extends tx_scheduler_Task {
    public function execute() {

        $connection = ftp_connect('ftp.software.ibm.com');
                    if (!$connection)
```

Any command-line input or output is written as follows:

```
Shell> apt-get install apache2-mpm-prefork libapache2-mod-php5 php5-gd
php5-mysql mysql-server-5.0
```

New terms and **important words** are shown in bold. Words that you see on the screen, in menus or dialog boxes for example, appear in the text like this: "clicking the **Next** button moves you to the next screen".

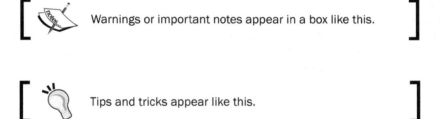

Warnings or important notes appear in a box like this.

Tips and tricks appear like this.

Reader feedback

Feedback from our readers is always welcome. Let us know what you think about this book— what you liked or may have disliked. Reader feedback is important for us to develop titles that you really get the most out of.

To send us general feedback, simply send an e-mail to feedback@packtpub.com, and mention the book title via the subject of your message.

If there is a book that you need and would like to see us publish, please send us a note in the **SUGGEST A TITLE** form on www.packtpub.com or e-mail suggest@packtpub.com.

If there is a topic that you have expertise in and you are interested in either writing or contributing to a book on, see our author guide on www.packtpub.com/authors.

Customer support

Now that you are the proud owner of a Packt book, we have a number of things to help you to get the most from your purchase.

Downloading the example code for the book

Visit http://www.packtpub.com/files/code/8488_Code.zip to directly download the example code.

The downloadable files contain instructions on how to use them.

Errata

Although we have taken every care to ensure the accuracy of our content, mistakes do happen. If you find a mistake in one of our books—maybe a mistake in the text or the code—we would be grateful if you would report this to us. By doing so, you can save other readers from frustration and help us improve subsequent versions of this book. If you find any errata, please report them by visiting http://www.packtpub.com/support, selecting your book, clicking on the **let us know** link, and entering the details of your errata. Once your errata are verified, your submission will be accepted and the errata will be uploaded on our website, or added to any list of existing errata, under the Errata section of that title. Any existing errata can be viewed by selecting your title from http://www.packtpub.com/support.

Piracy

Piracy of copyright material on the Internet is an ongoing problem across all media. At Packt, we take the protection of our copyright and licenses very seriously. If you come across any illegal copies of our works, in any form, on the Internet, please provide us with the location address or website name immediately so that we can pursue a remedy.

Please contact us at `copyright@packtpub.com` with a link to the suspected pirated material.

We appreciate your help in protecting our authors, and our ability to bring you valuable content.

Questions

You can contact us at `questions@packtpub.com` if you are having a problem with any aspect of the book, and we will do our best to address it.

1
Getting Started

Recently, the Internet has shifted from being a provider of mostly textual information to a rich media platform; delivering high quality audio, video, and more. This shift was pioneered by sites such as YouTube, Flickr, Last.fm, Facebook, and others. The availability of broadband and faster connection speeds, throughout the world, has aided this shift. This change has brought new challenges to content providers, as they now need to organize and deliver to the customer not only textual content, but all other forms of media. While textual information can be easily manipulated, multimedia objects are a lot harder to work with.

Traditional **Content Management Systems (CMS)** have focused on organizing and manipulating textual information, but modern systems have more support for multimedia. In this book, we will discover how to manage various forms of rich media content in TYPO3—one of the world's leading open source CMSs.

In this chapter, we will cover:

- ► Setting up a web server on Debian
- ► Setting up a multithreaded environment
- ► Setting up a web server on Windows
- ► Creating a scalable architecture
- ► Setting up an NFS share
- ► Setting up TYPO3
- ► Installing needed extensions
- ► Creating a template for a site

Introduction

Welcome to this book about the vast world of TYPO3 Multimedia! In this book, we will cover various topics that relate to manipulating multimedia objects in the TYPO3 content management system.

In this chapter, we will lay down some expectations for the rest of the book, and set up the environment that we will use for most of the examples used throughout the book.

Expectations and prerequisites

In order to get the most from this book, there are some expectations of prior knowledge and experience. It is assumed that the reader has a good understanding of TYPO3, which can be achieved by reading the introductory tutorials—*Inside TYPO3, TYPO3 Core API*, and *Modern Template Building guide*—essential to understanding how TYPO3 works. Basic TypoScript knowledge is required as well.

We will write several extensions in this book; however, we will omit a lot of the details about extension writing, focusing rather on the specifics of the extension. If you're new to extension development in TYPO3, you should look for resources on the subject on `www.typo3.org`. *TYPO3: Extension Development*, Dmitry Dulepov, Packt Publishing is an excellent book that covers all of the prerequisites and much more.

There are multiple ways to achieve anything in TYPO3. The best solution depends on the situation, and generally requires some compromises. This book cannot illustrate the best solution to every problem, but attempts to show various possibilities and approaches to problem solving using practical examples.

Most examples assume you have administrator access to the installation. If you are an editor or a designer, and have a restricted access to the system, you should skip the examples that pertain to developers, or ask your system administrator to provide you appropriate access.

Note on IDE

While all of the examples presented in this book can be completed using standard tools such as a web browser and a text editor, I highly recommend using an **Integrated Development Environment** (**IDE**) if you're serious about web development. IDE would save you time, boost your productivity, and provide insight into your application that is simply not possible with standard tools.

There are a variety of PHP IDEs available for various platforms and budgets. Popular products include Komodo IDE, Zend Studio, NetBeans, and Eclipse with PDT plugin. My weapon of choice is NuSphere PhpED, and you may see examples and screenshots throughout the book that make use of the PhpEd platform. The examples can be transposed to the IDE you're using, but this may require looking in the manual or searching online for the detailed description.

Setting up a web server on Debian

Before we start anything else, we need to set up a web server. The most common setup for TYPO3 is based on a LAMP stack (Linux, Apache, MySQL, and PHP), although other setups are supported as well. Next, we will install all the components required by TYPO3 on a Debian Linux server.

 Paths may vary depending on system and setup options.

Getting ready

Setting up a Debian server is very easy, because all the packages you need are available through **APT** (**Advanced Packaging Tool**). Make sure that the package lists are up-to-date by running:

```
Shell> apt-get update
```

How to do it...

Issue the following command while logged in as root:

```
Shell> apt-get install apache2-mpm-prefork libapache2-mod-php5 php5-gd
php5-mysql mysql-server-5.0
```

 At the time of writing, the latest stable version of Apache on Debian (Lenny) is 2.2.9, while PHP is 5.2.6, and MySQL is 5.0.51a. These versions meet the requirements of our system, and don't have any known bugs that prevent TYPO3 from working correctly.

How it works...

APT makes software maintenance easy, as all packages can be upgraded or removed through simple commands. You could install the packages from source, but it would make subsequent upgrades difficult. With APT, you can run the following to update the package cache information and upgrade your system:

```
Shell> apt-get update
Shell> apt-get upgrade
```

One could also use the short notation of this:
`apt-get update && apt-get upgrade`

It's highly recommended to do this on a regular basis to apply any security patches. But be careful—upgrades could break some functionality!

 Make sure you have a backup/failover plan in place before performing any upgrades.

There's more...

We can also install some other components to add additional functionality to our system.

ImageMagick

This line will install ImageMagick on your system.

```
Shell> apt-get install imagemagick
```

This installs ImageMagick—a powerful graphic processing program. TYPO3 works with GD and ImageMagick, and you can enable the use of ImageMagick in the Install Tool. As ImageMagick is an external program (unlike GD, which is a PHP extension), it is more efficient and feature-rich when it comes to image processing. Therefore, it's highly recommended that you install and enable it.

An alternative to ImageMagick is GraphicsMagick—a fork of ImageMagick with a more stable API. GraphicsMagick is also more efficient, and performs better than ImageMagick, especially on multi-core processors. No changes to TYPO3 are required to work with GraphicsMagick, and it can be utilized as soon as it is installed by using the following command:

```
Shell> apt-get install graphicsmagick
```

To verify that everything is functioning correctly, you can go into TYPO3 Install Tool (available when you install TYPO3 as described in recipe *Setting up TYPO3*), and select **Image Processing** to check the configuration, then run some tests, as shown on the following screenshot:

⌨ Current configuration

ImageMagick enabled: **0**
ImageMagick path: ()
ImageMagick path/LZW: ()
Version 5/GraphicsMagick flag:

GDLib enabled: **1**
GDLib using PNG:
GDLib 2 enabled: **1**
IM5 effects enabled: **0** (Blurring/Sharpening with IM 5+)
Freetype DPI: **72** (Should be 96 for Freetype 2)
Mask invert: (Should be set for some IM versions approx. 5.4+)

File Formats: **gif,jpg,jpeg,png**

ⓘ Testmenu

Click each of these links in turn to test a topic. **Please be aware that each test may take several seconds!:**

1: Reading image formats
2: Writing GIF and PNG
3: Scaling images
4: Combining images
5: GD library functions

Apache commands

Apache provides a few tools that significantly simplify maintenance tasks. Here are some useful commands:

```
Shell> a2enmod module_name
Shell> a2dismod module_name
```

The first command line (shown above) enables a module while the second command line disables a module (example: mod_rewrite).

```
Shell> a2ensite site_name
Shell> a2dissite site_name
```

The first command line enables a website configuration file while the second command line disables a website configuration file (example: default).

> Always put different site configurations in separate files. This way you can be sure that disabling a site configuration will only disable that website, and will not have any adverse effects on the other sites hosted on the server.

```
Shell> apache2ctl start
Shell> apache2ctl stop
Shell> apache2ctl restart
```

The commands you just saw are used to start, stop, or restart the server respectively. Make sure to restart the server after configuration changes, as they will not take effect (alternatively, you can reload the server).

There are many other resources online to help you set up and optimize the web server. One such resource that also gives some information specific to TYPO3 is `http://www.installationwiki.org/Typo3`.

See also

- ▸ *Setting up a multithreaded environment*
- ▸ *Creating a scalable architecture*
- ▸ *Setting up an NFS share*

Setting up a multithreaded environment

TYPO3 is an enterprise content management system, so it is **thread safe**—meaning two instances of the script can be executed simultaneously, and they will run in parallel without interfering with each other. Therefore, Apache can be set up with `mod_fcgid` and PHP processes will be allowed to run in parallel.

 This setup is not recommended if you have a server with only one or two core processor.

How to do it...

1. Install components of the server:

   ```
   Shell> apt-get install libapache2-mod-fcgid apache2-mpm-worker
   php5-cgi
   Shell> a2enmod actions
   Shell> a2enmod fcgid
   ```

2. Replace contents of `/etc/apache2/mods-available/fcgid.conf` with:

   ```
   <IfModule mod_fcgid.c>
     AddHandler fcgid-script .fcgi
     SocketPath /var/lib/apache2/fcgid/sock
     IPCConnectTimeout 60
     IPCCommTimeout 256
     BusyTimeout 256
     ProcessLifeTime 256
   </IfModule>
   ```

3. Modify site configuration, by default located in `/etc/apache2/sites-available/default`

4. Add the following to the virtual host definition:

```
Alias /fcgi-bin/ /var/www/fcgi-bin.d/
Action php-fcgi /fcgi-bin/php-fcgi-wrapper
```

5. Add the following lines to the directory definition for /var/www/:

```
AddHandler fcgid-script .php
FCGIWrapper /usr/bin/php-cgi .php
```

6. While there, modify the Options, adding +ExecCGI. Your final site configuration should look like this:

```
<VirtualHost *:80>
    ServerAdmin webmaster@localhost
    Alias /fcgi-bin/ /var/www/fcgi-bin.d/
    Action php-fcgi /fcgi-bin/php-fcgi-wrapper
    DocumentRoot /var/www/
    <Directory /var/www/>
        AddHandler fcgid-script .php
        FCGIWrapper /usr/bin/php-cgi .php
        Options Indexes FollowSymLinks MultiViews +ExecCGI
        AllowOverride None
        Order allow,deny
        allow from all
    </Directory>
</VirtualHost>
```

[Refer to the Apache manual for descriptions of some of the options listed above, as well as other configuration options.]

7. Create the executable link to PHP CGI module:

```
Shell> mkdir /var/www/fcgi-bin.d
Shell> ln -s /usr/bin/php5-cgi /var/www/fcgi-bin.d/php-fcgi-wrapper
```

How it works...

apache2-mpm-worker package, downloaded in the first command line call, is designed to run several threads simultaneously. PHP CGI binary is installed in the same statement.

We then enable the fcgid Apache module, and adjust its configuration. Most installations need to increase the timeout; otherwise, you will be looking at an Internal Server Error if the page rendering takes too long. To further complicate the diagnosis, timeouts are not recorded in logs. We increase the values of IPCConnectTimeout, IPCCommTimeout, and BusyTimeout, along with the ProcessLifeTime. Depending on your configuration, you may need to increase these values further.

Now, when a request comes in to Apache, the PHP CGI process will be launched to handle it. With multiple simultaneous requests, multiple processes will be launched, and run parallel to each other, handling individual requests.

 If you have multiple clients using this server, they can have separate PHP processes, and not interfere with each other (for security purposes). You can find more information on configuring this set up at `http://typo3.org/development/articles/using-php-with-mod-fcgid/`.

See also

▸ *Creating a scalable architecture*

▸ *Setting up an NFS share*

Setting up a web server on Windows

TYPO3 runs on a Windows server with IIS. This setup is less common, but supported. Most examples in this book assume you're running a Linux server.

If you want a development environment on your local computer running Windows, you can set up WAMP server. It is an all-in-one installer that can set up all the necessary components in minutes. Obviously, it will not be optimized for performance, but it will be enough to start experimenting with TYPO3. Just download the installation package, and run the executable file. It will guide you through the steps needed to complete the installation.

 Download WAMP distribution at `http://www.wampserver.com/en`.

An alternative to WAMP is XAMPP—another package containing Apache, MySQL, PHP, and Perl. Unlike WAMP, XAMPP is not specific to Windows platforms, and could be installed on a Mac, Linux, or Solaris system as well.

 Find out more about XAMPP at `http://www.apachefriends.org/en/xampp.html`.

How to do it...

1. Go to **Control Panel | Add or Remove Programs | Add/Remove Windows Components**, and check the box next to **Internet Information Services (IIS)** as shown in the following screenshot. Have your original installation CD handy, as you will probably be asked for it to complete the installation.

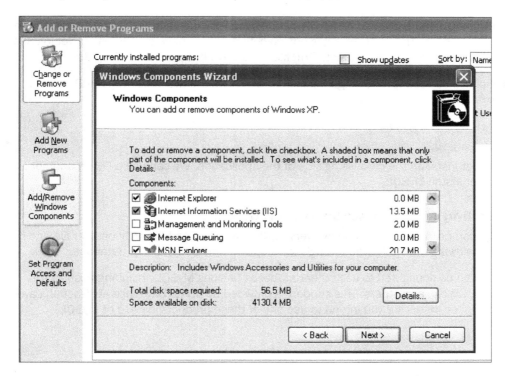

2. Download the TYPO3 source and dummy package, and extract them into `C:\Intepub\wwwroot`.

3. Download the installer binary package from `http://php.net`, and run it. Select the IIS CGI or Fast CGI module, and make sure that you install the complete package (including extensions).

4. Restart the web server, and proceed with TYPO3 installation.

How it works...

Windows web environment is powered by **Internet Information Services** (**IIS**). This component is available in most Windows systems, but not installed by default. In Step 1, we install this missing component. Once the installation is complete, our server is functional and capable of serving files over the Web.

At this point, if you browse to a PHP file on the server through a browser, you should see the PHP source code. The problem is it is not executing—that is because PHP is not yet installed, and IIS doesn't know how to handle PHP files. We solve this problem in Step 3.

Additional instructions for configuring PHP to run on IIS are available in the PHP manual: http://www.php.net/manual/en/install.windows.php

There's more...

We've just installed the processing side of the application. We can use a DB on another server, or install MySQL.

Installing MySQL database on Windows

MySQL can be installed on Windows very easily. Just download the MSI Installer file and run it. The install wizard will take you through the steps needed to install the database.

TYPO3 can be configured to use other databases besides MySQL, including PostgreSQL, MS SQL, Oracle, and others. This support is provided by DBAL (Database Abstraction Layer) extension, so install it if you intend to use one of these products instead of MySQL.

See also

 ▶ *Setting up TYPO3*

Creating a scalable architecture

In the previous examples, we've installed the database server on the same physical machine as the web server. Although a small website will perform just fine on a single server, larger sites will hit performance bottlenecks caused by limited capacity. A common industry solution to this problem is to place the web server on a different physical server from the database. This allows accommodation of future traffic increases by adding more processing servers.

As mentioned before, TYPO3 is thread-safe, so the processes running on one server will not interfere with processes on the other servers.

How to do it...

Once you have moved your database to a different server, you need to point TYPO3 to the new DB host. If you haven't installed TYPO3 yet, refer to the next recipe. Otherwise, select the **Admin Tools | Install** module in the TYPO3 backend, or if you don't have access to the backend yet, go to `http://example.com/typo3/install/` (replacing example.com with the domain name of your site).

Resolving missing ENABLE_INSTALL_TOOL file error

You may get an error, stating that the Install Tool has been locked due to missing `ENABLE_INSTALL_TOOL` file. This file is a security precaution, preventing anyone from potentially accessing system settings. If this file is present, it is removed after one hour of inactivity for the same reason. But there are several ways to recreate it. If you're logged in to the backend, the easiest way to create the file is to go to **User tools | User settings – [admin]**, and under **Admin functions** tab, click the button **Create Install Tool Enable File**:

If you don't have access to the backend, you can create the file manually using the following command line or a file explorer:

```
Shell> touch /var/www/typo3conf/ENABLE_INSTALL_TOOL
```

Once you have gained access to the Install Tool, go to **Basic configuration**, and adjust the database access information.

There's more...

You can now scale **horizontally,** by adding more processing servers accessing the same database. In this setup, storage becomes a problem. Luckily, most static files needed by TYPO3 are stored in the `fileadmin` folder that can be mounted from an external resource, such as **Network Attached Storage** (**NAS**). See the next recipe *Setting up an NFS share* to see how this can be accomplished.

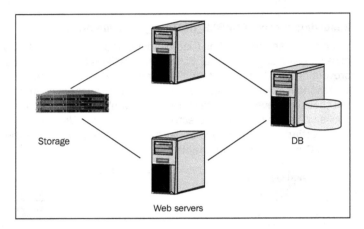

We have now arrived at a highly scalable set up. Should the traffic to the application increase, extra **nodes**—either web servers or database servers—can be added. This also allows for failover in case of hardware or software failure. These setups are more complex and are outside the scope of this book.

See also

▶   *Setting up an NFS share*

Setting up an NFS share

In the *Creating a scalable architecture* recipe, we arrived at a server architecture to support a website. That architecture required a separate storage, linked to processing servers over the network. In this recipe, we will cover how you could set up such NAS on a Debian Linux server with no special hardware.

How to do it...

1.   Run the following command to install all the required components for **Network File System** (**NFS**) sharing:

    ```
    Shell> apt-get install nfs-kernel-server nfs-common portmap
    ```

2. Edit /etc/exports file, and add the following line:

    /var/www/fileadmin 10.0.0.0/24(rw)

3. Run the following command to make the changes effective:

    Shell> exportfs -a

How it works...

You can fine tune the line in /etc/exports to fit your needs. Pay particular attention to access if you want your files to be secure. You could list individual servers as a comma-separated list, and give them explicit permissions to the shared folder.

The folder fileadmin will now be shared by other computers on the network, and could be accessed by several web servers in our scalable architecture. Changes to the TYPO3 code—such as installing extensions or changing configuration values—will still need to be done independently on each server, but all media files can be stored on the NFS share.

There's more...

In the following section we will see how we can mount a Network File System.

Mounting an NFS

You need to install similar tools—nfs-kernel-server, nfs-common, portmap—to mount the network file system correctly. Run the following command as a root user:

Shell> apt-get install nfs-common

After that, mount the shared folder on a different server with the following command:

Shell> mount -t nfs hostname:/nfs_folder /var/www/fileadmin

See also

> ▸ *Creating a scalable architecture*

Setting up TYPO3

We now have a web server running; so, we can install TYPO3.

How to do it...

1. Download the latest stable release, and a dummy package from http://typo3.org.

2. Read INSTALL.txt.

3. Extract all files to `/var/www`.

To ease upgrades in the future, or to run several TYPO3-driven sites from the same code base, you should extract the TYPO3 source package into a separate directory from the dummy package. For example, you could create a directory `src` under `/var/www`, and create a folder for each version of TYPO3 that you plan on using. Also, under `/var/www`, create a folder for each site you want to have on this server, and extract the dummy package into each folder. Next, create symbolic links for folders `misc`, `t3lib`, and `typo3` in the site folders, linking to the source package.

   ► `misc`:

   ```
   ln -s /var/www/src/typo3-4.3.0/misc /var/www/mysite/misc
   ```

   ► `t3lib`:

   ```
   ln -s /var/www/src/typo3-4.3.0/t3lib /var/www/mysite/t3lib
   ```

   ► `typo3`:

   ```
   ln -s /var/www/src/typo3-4.3.0/typo3 /var/www/mysite/typo3
   ```

When a new version is released, simply create a new folder for it, and change the links. If you realize that the new version is incompatible, you can quickly restore links to the old version.

4. Launch **1-2-3** installer. If you have a fresh new installation, simply go to `http://example.com/typo3/index.php`, and it will redirect you to the installer.

5. Enter your database information in Step 1. If you installed the database on the same host as the web server, enter `localhost` under address.

6. In Step 2, select an empty database where you would like the TYPO3 data to be stored, or create a new database. Make sure the database you choose to use is empty.

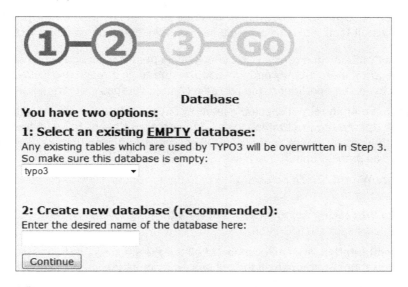

7. In the final step, TYPO3 will import the default data schema and records it needs to operate. You should now be able to log in to the TYPO3 backend.

 If the backend user account has not been created, you can access the Install Tool, and go to **Database Analyzer** to create the new backend user account.

How it works...

There are several ways to download the latest version of TYPO3 source and the dummy package. The best way to access both is to go to `http://typo3.org/` and click on **Download**. The source package contains all the TYPO3 core files needed for the system, while the dummy package helps create the needed directories and files specifically for your site.

Before you proceed with uploading the files to the web server, you must read the instructions in `INSTALL.txt`. Installation instructions change often and there may be components of the web server that are required in the future. Installation documentation covers all the nuances of installing the specific version you have just downloaded.

There's more...

After you have finished installing, explore the Install Tool fully, as it contains a full array of options you need to configure your system. Go to `http://example.com/typo3/install` to launch the Install Tool (replacing example.com with the domain name of your site).

- **Basic Configuration** runs a basic check of file permissions and server settings, and will report if there are any problems. Make sure to go through any issues, as they're likely to impact operations. You can also change database information here.

- **Database Analyzer** will check the integrity of your database schema. Click **COMPARE** under **Update required tables** to see if the database needs to be upgraded. Make sure that you do this after every TYPO3 source or extension upgrade. You can also delete all data, or import it again.

- **Update Wizard** should be used when you upgrade your TYPO3 source version—for example from 4.3 to 4.4.

- **Image Processing** will run a series of tests to check the ImageMagick, GD, or GraphicsMagick configuration.

- **All Configuration** gives an overview of all the system configuration variables available in the system. Go through all the options, and adjust the value to fit your system.

- **typo3temp/** gives statistics and lets you perform operations on temporary files created by TYPO3.

- **Clean up database** lets you clear cached image sizes.

- **phpinfo()** gives a standard PHP status report.

- **Edit files in typo3conf/** allows some basic edit operations on files in the `typo3conf` directory.

- **About** gives some general information about the use of the script, in greater detail than just described.

There is an excellent installation guide available from `http://dmitry-dulepov.com/e-books/typo3-installation-and-upgrade.html`. It covers setup instructions, as well as steps that need to be taken to optimize and secure the new installation.

See also

- *Installing needed extensions*
- *Creating a template for a site*

Installing needed extensions

Most of the power of TYPO3 comes from extensions. In fact, much of the system you have just installed is powered by extensions—these come packaged with the source, and are called **system extensions,** or simply **sysext**. You can find them under the `typo3/sysext` folder. These extensions have been deemed necessary for most installations, and many come preloaded by default. There are more extensions available through the TYPO3 Extension Repository (TER), and they can be installed as **local extensions**, and will reside under the `typo3conf/ext` folder. You can get a complete list at `http://typo3.org/extensions`.

As we will be dealing a lot with multimedia, we should install the **Digital Asset Manager** (**DAM**) extension. Its extension key is `dam`. While you can run a website without it perfectly well, a lot of the information provided in subsequent chapters will assume that you have a lot of media objects, and need an efficient way of organizing them. DAM is designed to do just that.

There are several ways to install extensions in TYPO3. Next, we will cover how you can install extensions using the Extension Manager—which is the simplest way to install extensions. For other possibilities, refer to the *There's more...* section further ahead. You may choose different options depending on the situation, so you should be familiar with all methods.

How to do it...

1. Go to **Admin Tools | Extension Manager**.

 If you've just installed the system, the Extension Manager is not configured for automatic extension retrieval. If it is already set up, skip to Step 7.

2. In the top-most selection box, choose **Settings** to go to the settings submodule.

 Terminology

A quick note about terminology: All options in the left frame of the backend menu are called **modules.** Some modules may have submodules—those are usually available in selection boxes at the top of the content frame. Refer to TYPO3 official documentation for an overview of the structure of the backend.

3. Under **Security Settings**, check the box if you want access to extensions that have not been reviewed. If you leave the box unchecked, and are unable to find some mentioned extensions, this would probably be the reason.

4. If you plan on uploading extensions to TER, then under **User Settings,** enter your TYPO3 account information. You can sign up for a free account at `http://typo3.org`.

5. Under **Mirror list**, select the mirror that is closest to you, or leave the recommended setting of random.

6. Scroll to the bottom and click **Update** to save your changes.

7. Go back to the submodule selector and choose **Import Extensions**.

8. In the **List or look up all extensions** box, type in **dam**.

9. In the list that appears, choose the **Media (DAM)** extension, and choose the **Import** button.

10. You will be notified of any **Dependency Error** that you can ignore or resolve.

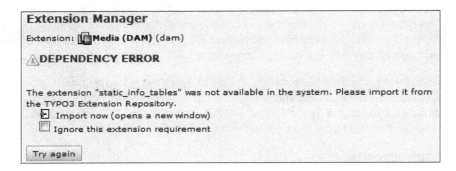

The **Extension Manager** will perform all the necessary database updates.

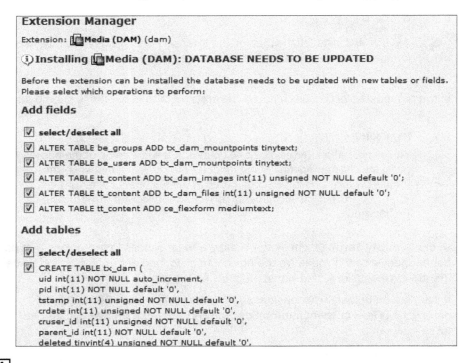

There's more...

In the following section we will cover other methods of importing extensions—from T3X files and code repositories.

Importing T3X files

Extensions are distributed and can be downloaded as files with T3X extension. You can download the files through the TER. Once you have the file, it can be imported through the **Import Extensions** submodule of the extension manager. The rest of the steps are the same as above.

Checking out unstable extensions

In between stable releases, unstable versions can be exported from repositories. These versions contain bug fixes and new features, but may not be fully tested, and therefore contain some problems. Here is how the latest revision of DAM can be checked out from the repository. Create a new folder under `typo3conf/ext/dam`, and in it, run the following command:

```
Shell > svn co https://svn.typo3.org/TYPO3v4/Extensions/dam/dam/trunk
```

This command assumes you have Subversion installed. If you don't, you will get an error. Subversion client can be installed through APT:

```
Shell> apt-get install subversion
```

If you're using Windows, you can use Tortoise SVN that is a graphical interface to the Subversion client. It integrates seamlessly into Windows Explorer and most commands can be accessed through right-click context menu. Go to `http://tortoisesvn.net/` to find out more about Tortoise SVN.

The rest of the steps for installation are the same as above.

Creating a template for a site

Our goal is to have a website for people to visit, and as such that website needs a frontend template where content will be displayed (TYPO3 can be used for other applications as well).

Getting ready

We will create a very basic template, which will allow us to see the results of the work in TYPO3 on the page. On a real project, you will probably be given a template by a designer.

Make sure to create a template directory under `fileadmin`, and create a file `mainTemplate.html` with the following contents:

```html
<!DOCTYPE html PUBLIC "-//W3C//DTD XHTML 1.0 Transitional//EN"
"http://www.w3.org/TR/xhtml1/DTD/xhtml1-transitional.dtd">
<html xmlns="http://www.w3.org/1999/xhtml">
<head>
<title>Site template</title>
</head>
<body>
<!-- ###DOCUMENT_BODY### begin -->
<div id="container">
    <div id="leftContent">
<!-- ###LEFT_COLUMN### -->
        Left Column Content
<!-- ###LEFT_COLUMN### -->
    </div>
    <div id="centerContent">
<!-- ###CENTER_COLUMN### -->
        Center Column Content
<!-- ###CENTER_COLUMN### -->
    </div>
    <div id="rightContent">
<!-- ###RIGHT_COLUMN### -->
        Right Column Content
<!-- ###RIGHT_COLUMN### -->
    </div>
    <div id="borderContent">
<!-- ###BORDER_COLUMN### -->
        Border Column Content
<!-- ###BORDER_COLUMN### -->
    </div>
</div>
<!-- ###DOCUMENT_BODY### end -->
</body>
</html>
```

Also, create a new CSS file in the same directory, called `mainStyle.css` with the following content:

```css
#container {
    width: 100%;
    height: 100%;
}

#leftContent {
    float: left;
    width: 200px;
    display: inline;
```

```
}

#centerContent {
    float: left;
    width: 500px;
    display: inline;
}

#rightContent {
    float: right;
    width: 200px;
}

#borderContent {
    float: right;
    width: 200px;
}
```

Case Sensitivity

Make sure you follow case sensitivity, as TypoScript code is case sensitive, and it doesn't see `mainStyle.css` as the same as `mainstyle.css`.

Come up with a convention for yourself. If you know all your names, follow camelCase, you will save yourself a lot of double checking and headaches when something doesn't work.

How to do it...

1. In the **Template** module, browse to the page you would like to be the root of the site. Create a new root template.

2. In the **Includes** tab, include the `styles.content` (default) static template.

Any page can be the root of a new site, even if it's within an already defined page tree structure. By default, templates propagate through the tree, but a new template record can be set as root:

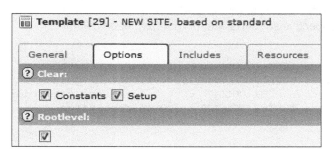

3. In the `setup` field, add the following code:

```
page = PAGE
page.typeNum = 0
page.10 = TEMPLATE
page.10 {
    template = FILE
    template.file = fileadmin/templates/mainTemplate.html
    workOnSubpart = DOCUMENT_BODY
    subparts.LEFT_COLUMN < styles.content.getLeft
    subparts.RIGHT_COLUMN < styles.content.getRight
    subparts.BORDER_COLUMN < styles.content.getBorder
    subparts.CENTER_COLUMN < styles.content.get
}
page.includeCSS.mainStyle = fileadmin/templates/mainStyle.css
```

How it works...

There is a lot that happens in just a few lines. Let's refresh your TypoScript knowledge.

`page=PAGE` creates a new top-level page object, and `page.typeNum=0` assigns a page type of 0 that is the default. So, when you go to the page with no `type` argument, this page object will be used.

 Other type numbers can be used to display content in a different form. For example, different type value can render a page for mobile device, for print, or even as XML for external applications, such as RSS feeds.

In the earlier code, `page.10=TEMPLATE` defines a content object at position 10 in the content object array. When the page is rendered, the content objects are each rendered in numerical order. `Page.10` is defined as a `TEMPLATE` content object, so it will take an HTML template file, and process it. Lines `template=FILE` and `template.file=fileadmin/templates/mainTemplate.html` define the location of the template file that will be loaded. `workOnSubpart=DOCUMENT_BODY` tells the page object to use the DOCUMENT_BODY subpart section of the template.

At this time, the template file will be loaded and output as it is. However, the following lines replace the respective subparts with output from each column:

```
page.10 {
    subparts.LEFT_COLUMN < styles.content.getLeft
    subparts.RIGHT_COLUMN < styles.content.getRight
    subparts.BORDER_COLUMN < styles.content.getBorder
    subparts.CENTER_COLUMN < styles.content.get
}
```

This is possible because we included the `styles.content` static template.

What will happen now is TYPO3 will get a list of all content elements in each column, and render them, that is, it will convert content into HTML. It will then place the resulting HTML code in place of the subparts.

The design in `mainTemplate.html` is very simple—just HTML. We want to apply some styling to that structure. Line `page.includeCSS.mainStyle=fileadmin/templates/mainStyle.css` includes our CSS file, which does just that.

There's more...

For more information about templates, you should read a detailed guide to templating in TYPO3: `http://typo3.org/documentation/document-library/tutorials/doc_tut_templselect/current/` (Modern Template Building). We will briefly go through a few more features.

Markers vs. Subparts

In the `mainTemplate.html` file, we have used four subparts. This lets us preview the file, and see exactly where the content will go once it is rendered. **Subparts** are defined by a unique marker, enclosed in HTML comment tags, and surrounding some text, as in:

```
<div><!-- ###TEMPLATE_SUBPART### --> Code that will be replaced <!--
###TEMPLATE_SUBPART### --></div>
```

Sometimes, you just want content to be inserted into a specific point, in such a case, you can use a marker. A **marker** is similar to a subpart, but exists by itself and doesn't reside in an HTML comment:

```
<div>###TEMPLATE_MARKER###</div>
```

Subparts are also used by extensions, where the subparts contain markers. This may not be clear at this point, but after working with a few templates you will grasp the difference.

Including JavaScript

To include JavaScript files, add the following lines to TypoScript:

```
page.includeJS.someCode = fileadmin/templates/someCode.js
```

See *TypoScript Reference* (*TSref*) for more options: `http://typo3.org/documentation/document-library/references/doc_core_tsref/current/`

2
Managing Digital Assets

In this chapter, we will cover:

- ▸ Setting up a file structure
- ▸ Setting up a filemount
- ▸ Setting up rights for backend users
- ▸ Setting up FTP access
- ▸ Setting up a category tree
- ▸ Creating a frontend upload form
- ▸ Debugging code
- ▸ Creating frontend user groups
- ▸ Creating frontend users

We will also look at digital asset management, why you may need it, and how to use it in TYPO3.

Setting up a file structure

When starting a new site, one needs to decide on the file structure that will be used. The specific directory tree will probably depend on the application and the type of information stored in those folders. But, there are certain ways by which TYPO3 can help you sort files, which should give you a guide as to how you should lay out the file tree.

Getting ready

First, you need to decide on the approach to the file structure.

- ▸ By user

  This is a common layout that's used in multiuser environments. Filemounts can be set up to limit the user to just a specific folder. We will examine how this can be done in the recipe *Setting up rights for backend users*.

- ▸ By user group

  This is similar to the previous setup, but more functional in team environments, where several users might share a job function. Filemounts can be set up for a group (content editor, publisher, videographer, and so on), and assigned to several users, who would then share access to files.

- ▸ By date

  If you have a lot of time-relevant content, storing by date makes sense. Then, selecting something from a specific day, month, or year becomes much easier using selections in DAM.

- ▸ By file type

  DAM can sort files by file type; so, your file tree should not focus on file types. However, you can separate the content by type—photos, videos, documents, and so on. Furthermore, you can break down the categories by specific topics that the files apply to. Note that specific topics can also be assigned to a file by use of categories, which we will cover later in this chapter.

How to do it...

Once you decide on the file structure you are going to use, you need to create the appropriate folders. We will use this structure for the next few examples. Folders can be created within TYPO3 and files can be uploaded through the same interface as well. In the following screenshot, you can see three icons—they are for New folder, Upload, and New file.

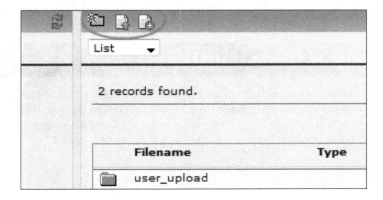

1. Click the **New folder** button in the upper left-hand corner of the **Media | File** module. In the **text** field, enter the folder name.

2. Click **Save**.

3. Click the **Upload file** button, or select the Upload sub-module from **Media | File** module.

4. Select the file or files that you want to upload. Note the folder name in the upper right-hand corner—this is where the uploaded files will be moved to.

5. Click **Upload**.

There are multiple options you can use to upload files onto the system.

Uploading multiple files

An alternative way to upload files is through a module, which can be accessed under **Media | File | Upload**. This module allows for multiple files to be selected for uploading.

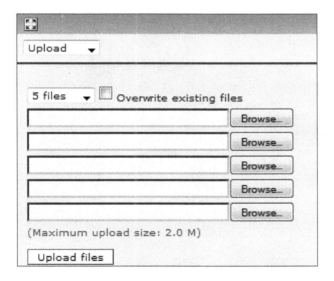

If you want to allow the new files to overwrite the existing files, check the **Overwrite existing files** checkbox. If it remains unchecked and there is a filename conflict, the new file will be appended a number to distinguish it from the item with the same filename.

Uploading through traditional file module

If you do not have DAM installed, you will have access to the traditional file module. It gives you access to the same functionality, letting users create new folders and upload files:

Click the **Upload files** button to upload one or more files into the current location. Click on the **New** icon to go to a form, which gives you an option to create new folders, among other possibilities, as shown in the following screenshot:

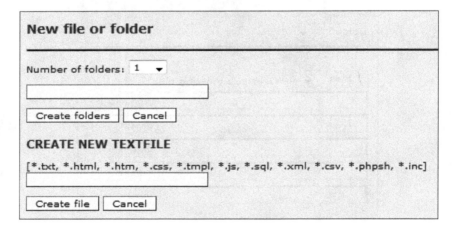

See also

▸ *Setting up rights for backend users*

Setting up a filemount

Filemounts limit a user to just a specific folder tree under the `fileadmin` directory. This is good for security purposes, as well as general usability in a multiuser environment. Instead of browsing through all the files available in the system, the user can be directed to just the files he/she needs to manipulate.

Getting ready

To set up filemounts, you must have a directory structure in place. For the recipe that follows, we will assume that we decided on a "by user" tree (see recipe *Setting up file structure*).

How to do it...

1. Use the **List** module and go to the root page of the site (**PID: 0**, usually the topmost node).
2. Click the **Create New Record** button.
3. Choose **Filemount**. You should see the following screen:

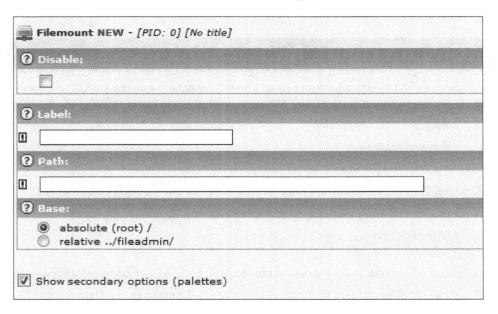

4. Fill in the required **Label** field. The **Label** field allows you to name the filemount to something you would remember, and could pick out from a list and know where it points.

5. Fill in the required **Path** field. The path refers to the file system path to the directory you want to set as the top level for the filemount.

> Examples for the path
>
> `/var/www/fileadmin/joe`
>
> `D:\www\fileadmin\susan`
>
> The path can be absolute, like the examples above, or relative to the `fileadmin` directory. Check an appropriate **Base** radio button depending on the path you provide.

There's more...

To use a filemount, just edit a backend user or backend user group.

See also

▶ *Setting up rights for backend users*

▶ *Setting up file structure*

▶ *Setting up FTP access*

Setting up rights for backend users

In this recipe, we will create a backend user, who will be able to log into TYPO3 and have limited rights, which would allow him or her to do his/her job without causing any deliberate or accidental damage to the system.

Getting ready

To limit a user to his/her folder, he/she must have a configured filemount. Make sure you have completed the *Setting up a filemount* recipe, and have correctly set up at least one filemount.

How to do it...

1. Under the **Admin tools | User Admin** module, click the button to create a new user.

2. Under the **General** tab, fill in the required fields—**Username** and **Password**.

3. Enter the user's name and e-mail address.

4. Under the **Access Rights** tab, select the modules that you would like the user or user group to see in the left frame.

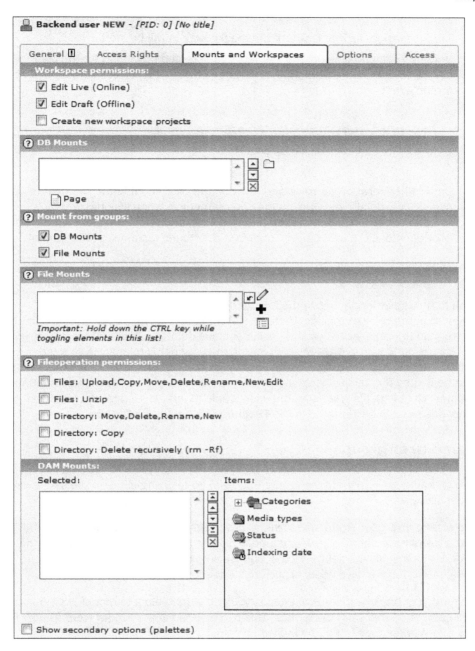

5. Under **DB Mounts**, select the top page of the branch to which the user should have access.

6. Under **DB Mounts**, make sure to also select the `Media` SysFolder that was created by DAM extension, as that is where the media records will be stored.

7. Under **File Mounts**, select the filemount you created previously for the user (or if you decided to set up the filemounts differently, choose the correct filemount combination for the user).

 You can select several filemounts if they apply to the user—use *Ctrl* + click on a PC or Command and click on a Mac.

8. Under **Fileoperation permissions**, select if the user should have the right to upload, copy, move, delete, rename, create new, and edit existing files (first option), unzip files (second option), create new, edit, move, delete, or rename directories (third option), copy directories (fourth option), or delete directories recursively (fifth option).

There's more...

Feel free to browse other options in the form and read the **Help** menu or the official documentation to see what they do. Under the **Mounts and Workspaces** tab are some options related to workspaces, which we will not focus on. If you have DAM installed, you will also get an option to set up **DAM Mounts**, giving the user rights to specific categories, media types, file statuses, and indexing dates (see the previous screenshot). Some other options that can be limited for specific users include display options (for example: maximum number of thumbnails in a list), file types that the user is able to upload, and much more. A lot of these options need to be set through the **TSconfig** field under the **Options** tab.

Backend user groups

If you have several users sharing the same basic set of rights, you can set up a backend user group, and add the user to the group. Backend groups can be set up the same way as individual users.

If you're setting up a user group, under the **Access Rights** tab, you can also specify which tables the users have rights to view and modify, as well as which exclude fields they have rights for. Exclude fields are set for tables, but users can be restricted from seeing and modifying them. You can give users explicit rights to these fields.

If a backend user has one or several groups, you can either select to mount DB mounts, file mounts, both, or neither from the groups. This can be done in the **Mount from groups** field of **Mounts and Workspaces** tab of the individual user.

Setting up FTP access

There are times when you need to allow FTP access to your users. There are plenty of FTP daemons to make it easy. However, you would have to set up individual users, and configure their restricted access. It is much better to leverage the backend user configuration already in TYPO3, and use it to provide basic FTP access to the same files accessible in the backend.

Getting ready

We will use Pure-FTPd daemon to provide FTP access. The steps below assume you are on a Debian system, and Pure-FTPd is available in package repositories. If its not, you would need to compile it from source.

How to do it...

1. Install Pure-FTPd, along with the MySQL authentication module.

    ```
    Shell> apt-get install pure-ftpd-common pure-ftpd-mysql
    ```

2. Open the MySQL configuration file (by default in `/etc/pure-ftpd/db/mysq.conf`). Edit the following values:

    - `MYSQLServer`: Point it to your MySQL server IP, or localhost
    - `MYSQLUser`: DB username
    - `MYSQLPassword`: DB password
    - `MYSQLDatabase`: Name of the DB that TYPO3 is using
    - `MYSQLCrypt`: "md5"
    - `MYSQLGetPW`: SELECT password FROM be_users WHERE username="\L" AND LEFT(username, 1) != '_' AND deleted=0
    - `MYSQLDefaultUID`: Web server user ID
    - `MYSQLDefaultGID`: Web server group ID
    - `MYSQLGetDir`:

      ```
      SELECT CONCAT('/path/to/fileadmin',file.path) AS Dir
      FROM be_users as user
      JOIN be_groups as ugroup ON user.usergroup=ugroup.uid
      JOIN sys_filemounts as file ON user.file_mountpoints=file.uid OR ugroup.file_mountpoints=file.uid
      WHERE user.username="\L" LIMIT 1
      ```

3. Replace `/path/to/fileadmin` with an actual path to the `fileadmin` directory on your server.

4. Create a new file `/etc/pure-ftpd/conf/ChrootEveryone` with content 'yes'.

5. Restart the Pure-FTPd daemon:

   ```
   Shell> /etc/init.d/pure-ftpd restart
   ```

6. Attempt to log in into FTP with one of the backend user credentials.

How it works...

When the user requests the FTP server and provides authentication values, Pure-FTPd will connect to the MySQL database, and issue queries to authenticate the user and, if successful, determine the starting directory. In the configuration file, we set some parameters to define this process. When the user is authenticated, the FTP daemon will establish connection with the MySQL database that we defined, select the TYPO3 database as we instructed, and issue the following query:

```
SELECT password FROM be_users WHERE username="\L" AND LEFT(username,
1) != '_' AND deleted=0
```

`\L` in this expression will be replaced with the username entered by the user and the query will return the password stored in the database for this user. We prevent usernames starting with underscores because those are usually used for system accounts, and user records that have been deleted. Password returned by this query will be encrypted, so we tell Pure-FTPd to encrypt the password used in the input prior to making the comparison.

If the user has been authenticated, we need to determine which directory they need access to. That is done by the second query:

```
SELECT CONCAT('/path/to/fileadmin',file.path) AS Dir
FROM be_users as user
JOIN be_groups as ugroup ON user.usergroup=ugroup.uid
JOIN sys_filemounts as file ON user.file_mountpoints=file.uid OR
ugroup.file_mountpoints=file.uid
WHERE user.username="\L" LIMIT 1
```

This will find one filemount from either this user's account, or the group account, and place the user into that directory upon login. This query also assumes filemount paths are relative to the `fileadmin` directory.

All file operations need to be made by the web server user—so that Apache can operate with them without running into permission issues. You can also modify specific permissions of new files and folders created through FTP.

Any files uploaded through FTP will not be indexed by the DAM. To have them indexed after they're uploaded, you can use the `dam_cron` extension to index all the new files on a schedule. See *Indexing downloaded files* recipe in Chapter 8 for more information

There's more...

There are a lot more options you can customize, based on your setup and business needs.

Debugging

If something is wrong in the configuration, the end user will not see any information as to what went wrong—he/she will simply be denied access. This makes it seem like there is an authentication issue, while it could be anywhere in the configuration. Luckily, Pure-FTPd logs all actions in the syslog, so you can refer to it for more information that should point you to the root of the problem. Syslog on Debian system is located in `/var/log/syslog`.

Different hosts

The FTP server doesn't have to be located on your processing server—in fact, it's better for security purposes to move it to a different host. The server can still access the same files, if you mount the `fileadmin` directory from an NFS share (see *Setting up an NFS Share* recipe in Chapter 1).

More options

There are other options that can be set. The manual covers them thoroughly, so refer to it for more information: `http://download.pureftpd.org/pub/pure-ftpd/doc/README.MySQL`.

See also

- ▶ *Setting up a filemount*
- ▶ *Setting up an NFS share*
- ▶ *Indexing downloaded files*

Setting up a category tree

Files can be sorted by categories. This provides another layer of classification for media assets, allowing them to be organized and grouped without changing their physical location. A common setup is to arrange the physical storage as we have—by user or by user group in order to make rights assignment easy, but setup a category tree by subject of the media content, to group similar files together. Here is an example:

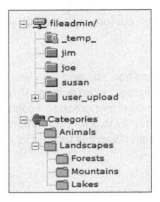

Getting ready

Category support is built in to DAM, but to ease category management you should install the extension `dam_catedit`. This extension provides full management capability optimized for DAM categories. We've covered how to install extensions in Chapter 1 in recipe *Installing needed extensions*, so refer back to it for a detailed description.

Once you have installed the extension, the **Categories** module will appear under **Media**.

How to do it...

1. Go to the **Media | Categories** module.

2. If there are no categories in the system yet, you will see only a top entry **Categories**. Click on it to bring up a context window, with the option to create a **New subcategory**. If there are already categories in the tree, click on any category to create a **New subcategory**.

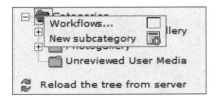

3. Fill in the form, making sure to enter a **Title**, as that's the only required field. Check that the **Parent category** is selected correctly.

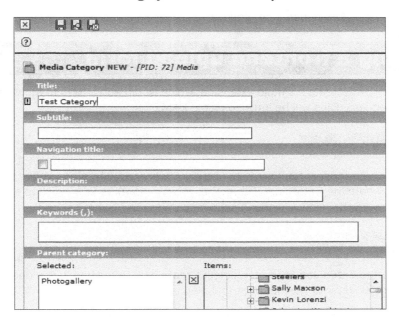

4. Save and close.

There's more...

Our recipe covered the creation of a category tree, but there are more uses for categories. Let's briefly touch on a few.

Associations

A file can only be in one folder, but the same file can be assigned to multiple categories. This creates enormous potential for media organization. Files can be classified according to their subjects. They can also be selected and sorted based on the categories assigned.

Photo galleries

Many photo gallery plugins use DAM categories as albums. We will configure one such gallery in Chapter 4. Other extensions use the same principle, and require a well-structured category tree to have a photo gallery based on images in the DAM.

More options

Other options available in the form include a **Description** field, **Subtitle**, **Keywords**, and access information. These fields are self-descriptive, and are described in the extension manual.

▸ *Creating a gallery using ce_gallery*

Creating a frontend upload form

In this recipe, we will create a simple extension, which would add a form to the website, and let users upload files. Files will be indexed by the DAM.

Getting ready

We will create the extension from scratch, and if you want to follow along, make sure to install Kickstarter to create the framework. Otherwise, you can download the finished extension—but make sure to review the *How it works...* section to understand what happens in the code.

How to do it...

1. Under the **Extension Manager**, select **Create new Extension**. If you don't see the option, Kickstarter has not been installed.

2. Under **General Info**, click the plus icon (**+**), and fill in the basic information. Name the extension **User Upload**.

3. Under **Dependencies**, enter **dam**. When the extension is installed, Extension Manager will check the presence of DAM, and proceed only if DAM is present and installed. Likewise, Extension Manager will not allow DAM to be uninstalled as long as our extension is still installed.

4. Click the plus icon next to **Frontend Plugins**. Check the box that generates the uncached USER_INT object. Leave other options as default.

Frontend Plugins

Create frontend plugins. Plugins are web applications running on the website itself (not in the backend of TYPO3). The default gue: shop, rating feature etc. are examples of plugins.

Enter a title for the plugin:

| User Upload | [English] |

☑ By default plugins are generated as cachable USER cObjects. Check this checkbox to generate an uncached USER_INT cObject.

5. Click the plus icon next to the Static TypoScript code, and name it **user_upload**. Enter the code from file `static/default/setup.txt` of extension `dam_user_ upload`, which can be downloaded from the book site.

6. Click **View result**, and write the generated files to the default directory.

7. Edit `ext_emconf.php`, look for the parameter `uploadfolder` in the `$EM_CONF[$_ EXTKEY]` array, and set it to 1.

8. Replace the contents of `pi1/class.tx_damuserupload_pi1.php` with contents of its namesake from `dam_user_upload.t3x`, downloaded from the book site (`http://www.packtpub.com/files/code/8488_Code.zip`).

9. Create the file `class.tx_damuserupload_feindexing.php` in the root of the extension with contents of its namesake from `dam_user_upload.t3x`, downloaded from the book site.

10. Create a new folder in the extension directory and name it `res`. Resource files (templates, images, JavaScript, CSS) should go here. Create a new file `template.html` with contents of its namesake from `dam_user_upload.t3x`, downloaded from the book site.

11. Install the newly created extension.

12. In the **Page** module, create a new page, and create a new content element on it of type **General Plugin**.

13. Select **User Upload** under the list of plugins. Preview the page, and you should see a form on the page. If you fill it out correctly, it will upload your file to `fileadmin/uploads/tx_damuserupload`.

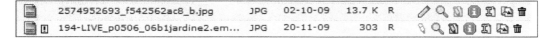

How it works...

We will go over each function to see what they do, and how they work.

main()

When a plugin is present on the page, the `main` function of the `tx_damuserupload_pi1` class is called when the page is rendered. The `$conf` parameter passed to the function contains the TypoScript configuration array, in our case from `plugin.tx_damuserupload_pi1`. What happens from that point on is up to the plugin. At the end, the main function should return the HTML output, which will be inserted into the page at the point where the plugin was called.

Remember markers and subparts? This is one of the instances where they come into play. The HTML output of a plugin is most likely going to replace a marker or a subpart—if called from TypoScript, or if the plugin was included in the **Page** module. Regardless, the plugin output is unlikely to be on a page by itself, and needs to be within a larger template. Markers and subparts, which are substituted by TYPO3 make it possible.

Let's examine the code line by line as it is executing.

Our plugin will be a USER_INT object, so it will not be cached with a page, but included every time. Therefore, we set the class variable to indicate this:

```
$this->pi_USER_INT_obj = 1;
```

We do this because the form substitutes some values based on the user who is logged in. If you look in ext_localconf.php, you will see this line:

```
t3lib_extMgm::addPItoST43($_EXTKEY, 'pi1/class.tx_damuserupload_pi1.
php', '_pi1', 'list_type', 0);
```

It adds the plugin information to the static template, so that when the plugin is called to render on a page, TYPO3 knows where to look for the code. Note that the last parameter is set to 0. The function definition states that if the last parameter–$cached–is set as USER, content object (cObject) is created, otherwise, a USER_INT object is created. We are creating a USER_INT object, so that is the reason for its value.

 Kickstarter took care of everything for us in this case, but it's important to understand what it did in case you want to make some changes later.

Next, we check for the presence of POST parameters sent to the script. If they are not present, it means that we need to show the user a form for uploading files. If they are present, then the form was submitted and we need to process it.

```
if (t3lib_div::_POST()) {
    $input = t3lib_div::_POST('tx_damuserupload_pi1');
    $content .= $this->uploadFile($input['title'], $input['author'],
$input['description']);
        }
else {
    $content .= $this->getForm();
}
```

Always use TYPO3's API function for accessing GET and POST parameters! These functions are a first line of defense against malicious values sent to the script. Use `t3lib_div::_GET()` to access GET variables, `t3lib_div::_POST()` to access POST variables, and `t3lib_div::_GP()` to get a value from either POST or GET, with preference to POST values.

That being said, you should always perform the necessary checks before using the values in your application, especially, if they are sent to the database. If the parameter should be a number, use `t3lib_testInt()` to see if it is indeed a number or PHP `intval()` function to convert into an integer. If the parameter should be a number within a certain range, use the `t3lib_div::intInRange()` function. If the input is a string, make sure it's quoted by using the `$GLOBALS['TYPO3_DB']->fullQuoteStr()` function to escape the value.

See `t3lib/class.t3lib_div.php` and `t3lib/class.t3lib_db.php` for the descriptions of these and other useful functions.

getForm()

The `getForm` function takes a template file, replaces a few markers, and returns the HTML output ready to be returned to the browser. For more information about how markers and subparts work, refer back to recipe *Creating a template for a site* from Chapter 1.

First, we get the template file content:

```
$templateFile = $this->cObj->fileResource($this-
    >conf['templateFile']);
```

Path to the template file is stored in `$this->conf['templateFile']`, which corresponds to `plugin.tx_damuserupload_pi1.templateFile`. This value could be different for different websites, different pages in the page tree, or even different elements on the page. Using the TypoScript value allows for maximum flexibility of the plugin.

We then extract the subpart `###FORM###` out of the entire template. Variable `$template` now contains the HTML within the subpart tags.

```
$template = $this->cObj->getSubpart($templateFile, '###FORM###');
```

The function then proceeds to replace the markers within the `$template` with content.

```
$markers['###LINKBACK###'] = $this->pi_getPageLink($GLOBALS['TSFE']-
    >id);
$markers['###MAXFILESIZE###'] = t3lib_div::getMaxUploadFileSize() *
    1024;
$markers['###AUTHOR###'] = $GLOBALS['TSFE']->fe_user->user['name'];
$markers['###EXTENSIONS###'] = str_replace('.', '', $this-
    >conf['allowedExtensions']);
```

We use the `pi_getPageLink` function (available from the `tslib_pibase` class) to get the link to the current page. We get the maximum allowed upload size through the `t3lib_div::getMaxUploadFileSize()` function, and convert it into bytes by multiplying the result by 1024. If a user is logged in to the frontend, then the user's name is available in the `$GLOBALS['TSFE']->fe_user->user['name']` variable. Otherwise, the variable will be empty. Finally, we display a list of allowed extensions, which again could vary depending on the use of the plugin, and could be set in TypoScript.

Finally, we substitute the markers with content, and return the resulting HTML:

```
return $this->cObj->substituteMarkerArrayCached($template, $markers);
```

uploadFile()

The `uploadFile` function processes the form results, handling file upload and indexing.

First, we gather information about the location of the file:

```
// Relative directory for user uploads
$relativeDirectory = $GLOBALS['TYPO3_CONF_VARS']['BE']['fileadminDir']
    . 'uploads/tx_damuserupload/';
// Full directory to user uploads
$uploadDirectory = t3lib_div::getIndpEnv('TYPO3_DOCUMENT_ROOT') .
    t3lib_div::getIndpEnv('TYPO3_SITE_PATH') . $relativeDirectory;
```

`$GLOBALS['TYPO3_CONF_VARS']['BE']['fileadminDir']` contains the path to the `fileadmin` folder—usually just `fileadmin/`, but the value can be different in different installations. Our folder is under `fileadmin/uploads/tx_damuserupload`—this is where the uploaded file should be moved. The folder is created when the extension is installed, and the value `$EM_CONF['dam_user_upload']['uploadfolder']` controls that behaviour. See Step 7 in *How to do it...* section for more information.

Next, we perform basic checks to see that everything is ready for file operations:

```
if(!is_dir($uploadDirectory)) {
```

checks that the upload directory exists—and wasn't deleted after it was created.

```
else if(!is_writable($uploadDirectory)) {
```

checks that the directory is writable by the server. If it's not, we will not be able to move the uploaded file there.

```
else if(!in_array(strtolower(strrchr(basename($_FILES['tx_
    damuserupload_pi1_file']['name']), '.')),
    t3lib_div::trimExplode(',', $this->conf['allowedExtensions'],
        TRUE))) {
```

checks that the uploaded file has an extension we have explicitly allowed to be uploaded.

For better security, check the file MIME type, and make sure it matches the used extension. We will leave this change as an exercise for the user.

In case any of the conditions are not met, an error message is sent to the browser. If everything is set, we proceed to choose a name for the uploaded file:

```
$i = 0;
do {
    $i++;
    $filename = t3lib_div::shortMD5($i . $GLOBALS['TSFE']->fe_user-
>user["uid"] . $_FILES['tx_damuserupload_pi1_file']['name']) . '_' .
        $_FILES['tx_damuserupload_pi1_file']['name'];
}
while(file_exists($relativeDirectory . $filename));
```

We use a hash to make the filename unique. In case the file already exists, we repeat the process using a different hash until we find an unused filename.

Finally, we move the file from its temporary location to the upload directory, and index it:

```
if (move_uploaded_file($_FILES['tx_damuserupload_pi1_file']['tmp_
    name'], $uploadDirectory . $filename)) {
    $uid = $this->indexFile($relativeDirectory . $filename, $title,
        $author, $description);
    $content .= '<b>Success:</b> The file <i>' . basename($_FILES['tx_
        damuserupload_pi1_file']['name']) . '</i> has been uploaded.';
}
```

indexFile()

Here, we initialize the indexing class, and run the indexing process. Indexing is needed to create a DAM record associated with the file.

```
$pid = tx_dam_db::getPid();
$time = $GLOBALS['EXEC_TIME'];
```

We gather two parameters from the indexing function—the PID of the page where the record will be stored (can be easily found using `tx_dam_db::getPid()`), and the time when the record was created.

 Typical function to use to get the Unix timestamp in PHP is `time()`. However, when used repeatedly, it causes a small performance drop. TYPO3 stores the time the script started executing in a global variable `$GLOBALS['EXEC_TIME']`, which is much faster to access than the `time()`.

We then instantiate the indexing class and run the indexing function:

```
$index = t3lib_div::makeInstance('tx_damuserupload_feindexing');
$index->init();
$index->initEnabledRules();
$index->setRunType('auto');
$meta = $index->indexFile($path, $time, $pid, $title, $author,
    $description);
```

Use `t3lib_div::makeInstance()` function instead of PHP new keyword to instantiate classes. This allows extensions to extend classes using XCLASS and have the extended class used instead of the original.

TYPO3 4.3 also supports **singletons**—meaning that regardless of how many times a class is instantiated, the same instance is returned every time. This saves a lot of memory in cases where the object doesn't need to have its own identity. To declare the class as singleton, it needs to implement the `t3lib_Singleton` interface:

```
class tx_myClass implements t3lib_Singleton {
...
}
```

Unfortunately, DAM's `tx_dam_indexing` class only works with a backend user logged in. As we are creating a form that will be used by frontend users, we need to rewrite some of the default functionality. Class `tx_damuserupload_feindexing` extends `tx_dam_indexing`, and replaces the function `indexFile` with a simplified version. We will not go into it in detail, but the only major changes are the function parameters which are stored in the fields list:

```
$meta['fields']['title'] = !empty($title) ? $title : $meta['fields']
    ['title'];
$meta['fields']['creator'] = !empty($author) ? $author :
    $meta['fields']['creator'];
$meta['fields']['description'] = !empty($description) ? $description :
    $meta['fields']['description'];
```

And the record is created directly in the database, bypassing the **TYPO3 Core Engine** (**TCE**):

```
function insertUpdateData($meta) {
    $meta = tx_dam_db::cleanupRecordArray('tx_dam', $meta);
    unset($meta['uid']);
    $res = $GLOBALS['TYPO3_DB']->exec_INSERTquery('tx_dam', $meta);
    return $GLOBALS['TYPO3_DB']->sql_insert_id($res);
}
```

There's more...

One useful extension of this concept is a workflow. An uploaded item can be attached to a workflow, and backend users will have to take action on it. An example application of this is having a backend user approve a file before it is shown on the site. Take a look at extensions `sys_workflows` and `sys_todos`, available from the TER.

Another extension you can use is `fileupload`. It works the same way, but doesn't use DAM for indexing.

See also

- ► *Creating frontend users*
- ► *Debugging code*

Debugging code

In the *Creating a frontend upload form* recipe, we went through the execution of the script line by line. When writing your own code, you would probably want the same benefit, giving you the ability to go through execution line by line, and seeing exactly what is happening. This functionality is provided by **debuggers**.

There are several debuggers available for PHP for any platform. Most debuggers are bundled with an IDE, so that you can use them together. For example, NuSphere PhpEd comes with DBG debugger, which we will make use of in this recipe.

Getting ready

This recipe assumes you have NuSphere PhpEd installed on your Windows computer. If you don't—skip ahead to the *There's more...* section for general tips on using debuggers, which you can then apply to a debugger of your choice.

[For more information about NuSphere PhpEd, go to
`http://www.nusphere.com/`.]

How to do it...

1. Go to `C:\Program Files\nusphere\phped\debugger\server` (or equivalent installation path).
2. Select the directory based on your web server (for example, if you're using WAMP, go to `Windows\x86`), and select the extension for your version of PHP.

3. Copy the `dll` file to the PHP extensions folder (in a default WAMP installation, `C:\wamp\bin\php\php5.x.x\ext`).

4. Enable the extension by adding the following lines to `php.ini`:

```
extension=php_dbg.dll
[debugger]
debugger.enabled=On
debugger.profiler_enabled=On
```

There's more...

Instructions for other platforms and other debuggers and systems are similar. Refer to the installation manual for specific steps on how to get the debugger working on your system.

Once installed, you can run the code through the debugger and set breakpoints where execution should pause, giving you an overview of the state of all variables.

One powerful function that the DBG debugger enables is the `DebugBreak();`. When placed anywhere within a program, it causes the execution to pause, and jumps into the IDE for debugging. This is extremely useful when you want to debug a state of the application (such as TYPO3) that requires authentication, complex parameters, or session variables. The following screenshot shows how to place `DebugBreak();` in between code:

When the execution stops on a breakpoint, we can get an overview of all the variables available—both local to our class and function, and global to the script. You can even change the value of any variable to a different value "on the fly". You can examine the call stack—the path the execution took to reach the breakpoint. Furthermore, you can go back in the stack to trace the variables to their initialization or instantiation, or step forward and observe the state of the application change with every line of code. The following screenshot shows how a **Call Stack** looks for our extension `dam_user_upload` we created in recipe *Creating a frontend upload form*:

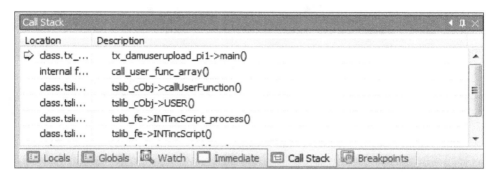

Debuggers can be installed on hosts other than your localhost, allowing you to use development environments closely matching your final production environment to debug your code.

Creating frontend user groups

Most websites have registration that gathers users' information and gives them access to certain functionality of the site—such as commenting, rating, or purchasing products. But suppose you would like to have several different groups of users, perhaps with different access rights? TYPO3 allows that—in fact, user groups are just another record that can be created.

How to do it...

1. In the **Web | Page** module, click on the parent page icon, and select **New**.

2. In the page wizard, select **SysFolder** as the page type (also known as record storage page).

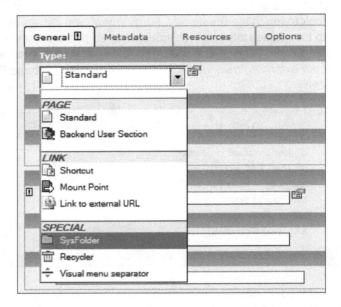

3. Switch to **Web | List** module, and in the newly created **SysFolder**, create a new record of type **Website usergroup**.

4. Fill in the group title that you would like to use to identify the group. For a description of the other options, refer to the official documentation.

See also

▶ *Creating frontend users*

Creating frontend users

Frontend users are also just records in TYPO3, just like everything else. However, you don't want to create the frontend users manually, especially if you have a large site with a lot of users. Luckily, there are extensions that make this operation easy to perform. We will install the extension `sr_feuser_register` and configure it to register users.

How to do it...

1. Install the `sr_feuser_register` extension. Refer to the Chapter 1 recipe *Installing needed extensions* for a reminder of how the extension can be installed.

2. Insert a static template. Modify the template record for the site, and under the **Includes** tab choose to include **FE User Registration** static TypoScript, either CSS-styled or old-style.

3. Insert the plugin on a page. Refer to the manual for possible codes. The plugin will render with the default template, which you have the option to change.

There's more...

In the previous recipe, *Creating frontend user groups*, we created several user groups. But how would users register into the various groups? This is actually simple—it only requires several pages with different instances of the plugin. Depending on which page the users use to register, they will be registered into different user groups. You would probably want to limit access to the different pages to prevent unauthorized access. You could also write a custom extension to change the user's user groups based on some parameters, but we will leave it as an exercise for you, the reader.

See also

▸ *Creating frontend user groups*

3
Operating with Metadata in Media Files

As great as modern technology is, computers are not yet able to look inside media files to describe them. Although there is some advancement, such as facial recognition technology, we still have to rely on metadata to describe files. In this chapter, we will learn about the major types of metadata, how it can be inserted in files, and how it can be extracted and used for content management in TYPO3.

In this chapter, we will cover:

- ▶ Inserting metadata into images
- ▶ Extracting metadata from images
- ▶ Inserting metadata into audio
- ▶ Extracting metadata from audio
- ▶ Extracting metadata from PDF

Inserting metadata into images

A lot of the images already have **metadata**. Most digital cameras record their settings at the time of capture (such as ISO setting, white balance, resolution, as well as camera model, firmware version, and more); along with image specific information (shutter speed, aperture, focal distance, use of flash, and so on). If an image is created using a software package, it usually saves some settings of its own, like software name, version, license key holder information, and more. So when you open an image, don't be surprised if it already has plenty of metadata in it.

How to do it...

In this section, you will see how we can insert metadata in Windows as well as Photoshop.

In Windows

To view the metadata stored in an image, and modify it if necessary, right-click on a file and select **Properties**. Under the **Details** tab, you will see all the available fields:

In Photoshop

Open the image, and under **File** menu, choose **File Info** You will be presented with the following screen:

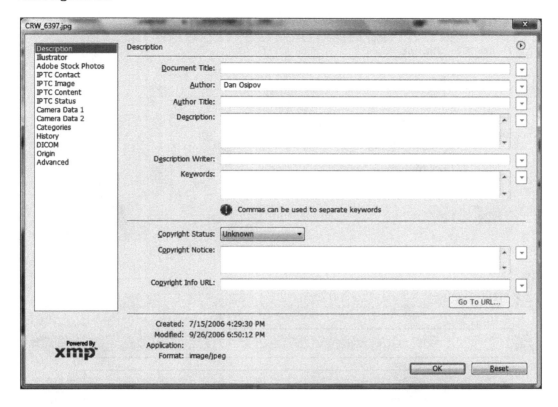

You now have access to all the fields of the metadata.

Extracting metadata from images

Extracting metadata from images, when they are uploaded, is very easy. Extension `cc_metaexif` in combination with DAM handles all the work for you.

How to do it...

1. Install `cc_metaexif`. Extension `cc_metaexif` is a service extension that is executed when new files are uploaded. It parses the metadata stored in the EXIF and IPTC sections of the image file, and stores this data in the DAM record associated with the image file.

2. To test how the extension is working, upload an image with modified metadata. You should see the metadata used in DAM fields, such as **Title**, **Description**, and **Copyright** owner.

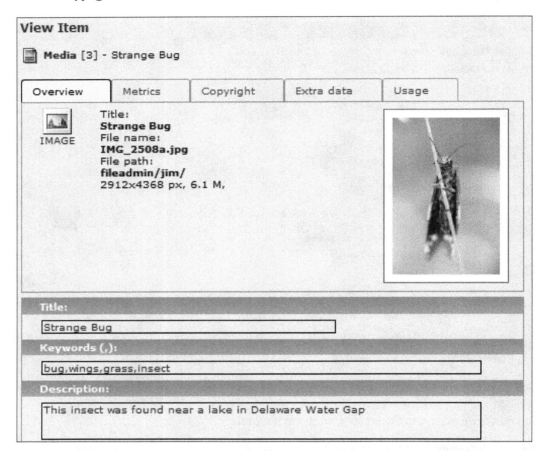

If you click on the **Extra data** tab, you will get access to raw data as it was imported from the file. Most of it probably didn't match any of the DAM fields, so remained unparsed. You can still make use of it by writing custom extensions that can manipulate this data and make use of it for your particular purpose. We will cover this later on in the book.

How it works...

Services are called upon a specific action. In this case, the service is called when a new file is indexed. It's only executed if the file is of a specific type, and if the system is capable of certain actions.

Let's look at how `cc_metaexif` works in detail. Open `ext_tables.php` in the extension folder. You can see that it defines three services. We'll examine the middle one:

```
t3lib_extMgm::addService($_EXTKEY,  'metaExtract'
    /* sv type */,  'tx_ccmetaexif_sv2' /* sv key */,
    array(

        'title' => 'EXIF extraction',
        'description' => 'Extract EXIF data from images'.
            'by PHP function "exif_read_data".',

        'subtype' => 'image:exif',

        'available' => function_exists('exif_read_data'),
        'priority' => 60,
        'quality' => 50,

        'os' => '',
        'exec' => '',

        'classFile' =>
            t3lib_extMgm::extPath($_EXTKEY).
            'sv2/class.tx_ccmetaexif_sv2.php',
        'className' => 'tx_ccmetaexif_sv2',
    )
);
```

The file `ext_tables.php` is called upon TYPO3 initialization, so this code is executed before any request is handled. The `addService` function of class `t3lib_extMgm` is called, and it adds the declared service to the service listings array, so that it can be called later. This type of service is **metaExtract**, which is utilized by the DAM, and the service key is `tx_ccmetaexif_sv2`. The last parameter is the configuration for the service, which is of most interest to us.

 Service keys must start with `tx_` or `user_`.

The `title` and `description` fields are self explanatory. `subtype` is not specifically defined, but is analyzed by each specific service type. In this case, it can either be a media type or a list of file extensions to parse. `available` field contains a simple check for availability of the service. Common uses are to check for the existence of a PHP function.

Parameters `priority` and `quality` define the precedence for a service. Here is what the TYPO3 official documentation says about the two parameters:

> *The priority is used to define a call order for services. The default priority is 50. The service with the highest priority is called first. The priority of a service is defined by its developer, but may be reconfigured. It is thus very easy to add a new service that comes before or after an existing service, or to change the call order of already registered services.*

> *The quality should be a measure of the worthiness of the job performed by the service. There may be several services who can perform the same task (e.g. extracting meta data from a file), but one may be able to do that much better than the other because it is able to use a third-party application. However if that third-party application is not available, neither will this service. In this case TYPO3 can fall back on the lower quality service which will still be better than nothing. Quality varies between 0-100.*

Fields `os` and `exec` can be used to restrict the service to a certain operating system, or a system that can execute a specific external program. `os` can be set to either `UNIX` for *nix systems, `WIN` for Windows, or left blank for no restriction. `exec` can contain an absolute path to a program, or just a program name.

There's more...

In this section we will see how to change the priority of services and how to install exiftags program required by the `tx_ccmetaexif_sv3` service.

Service priority

Suppose you want to change the priority of one of the services. Perhaps, the exiftags program exists on your system, but it's very resource hungry for one reason or another, and you would like to lower the priority of the service. Add the following to `typo3conf/localconf.php`:

```
$TYPO3_CONF_VARS['T3_SERVICES']['metaExtract'][ 'tx_ccmetaexif_sv3']
    ['priority'] = 20;
```

If you would like to turn off the service that gets the IPTC data, insert the following:

```
$TYPO3_CONF_VARS['T3_SERVICES']['metaExtract'][ 'tx_ccmetaexif_sv1']
    ['enable'] = false;
```

Exiftags

`tx_ccmetaexif_sv3` service depends on the external program exiftags. This program can be installed to make use of that service.

```
Shell> apt-get install exiftags
```

Also, refer to the official TYPO3 documentation for a description of services API and more options.

See also

- ▶ *Processing audio using a service*
- ▶ *Converting video into FLV upon import*
- ▶ *Converting audio using services*

Inserting metadata into audio

The most common format for audio metadata is ID3. There are two versions in use today, and you will probably see references to them as ID3v1 and ID3v2. Most software packages are able to read both.

 Audio metadata can sometimes be used to describe the characteristics of the audio stream used by audio players and decoders. We do not use this definition. Instead, we refer to the information about the file—similar to metadata in images.

How to do it...

Most music players give an option to modify the ID3 tags. You can also edit it in Windows, much in the same way as image metadata:

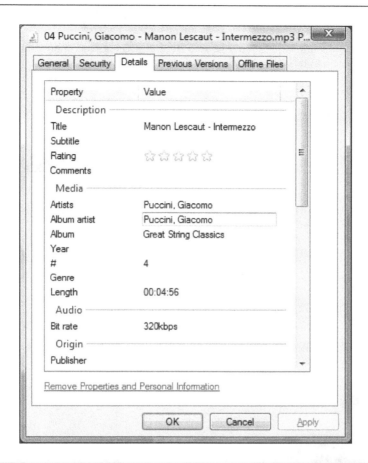

Extracting metadata from audio

In Chapter 7, we will create a service that will handle audio files and extract ID3 tags. If you've jumped ahead and created the service already, here is how you can utilize it. As always, there are several methods for accomplishing anything, and you can jump to the *There's more...* section to see another extension that extracts the ID3 metadata.

How to do it...

1. Install the `cc_meta_audio` extension. Refer to Chapter 1 for information on how to do that. Alternatively, you can skip ahead to Chapter 7 and follow the recipe for creating this extension.

2. Upload an audio file. Verify that ID3 tags exist in the file, and upload it. The service will be executed automatically upon file indexing.

To double-check, upload an audio file with ID3 tag, and check that they all show up in the **Extra data** tab of the file info:

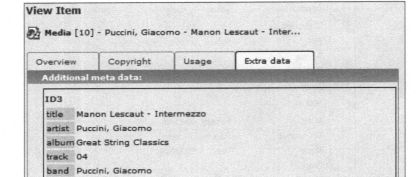

There's more...

Another extension that allows the extraction of audio and video metadata is `ma_meta_audiovideo`. This extension depends on an external program `mplayer`, which we can install using APT:

```
Shell> apt-get install mplayer
```

See also

▶ *Processing audio using a service*

Extracting metadata from PDF

By now, you probably see a pattern regarding embedding and extracting metadata in various file types. We will cover one more format—PDF, which is a format most often used for documents shared on the Web. You are likely to read this book in its PDF version, and even if you don't, it is available in PDF format. The PDF contains some metadata that is standard for all files of the type—title, description, author, date of creation, and more. This metadata can be embedded when the file is created in Adobe Acrobat or other application capable of writing PDF files.

How to do it...

1. Install the `cc_metaexec` extension.

2. Install `pdfinfo`. This utility can be installed on both Windows and Linux machines. We will install it on a Debian server using APT:

    ```
    Shell > apt-get install xpdf
    ```

    This command will install `pdfinfo`, along with other related tools.

 In Debain, the `pdfinfo` tool is hidden inside a different package. This may be the case for your operating system as well. You may need to search package descriptions and lists to see where `pdfinfo` could be hiding.

3. You can now check if the program is functioning properly, and TYPO3 can make use of it. Go to **Media | Tools | Services Info** submodule. You will see a list of all external services that DAM can make use of, and whether they are installed and available or not.

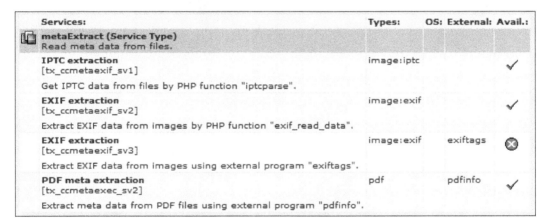

4. Once installed, it will take care of extracting metadata from PDF files that are uploaded or indexed by DAM.

4
Rendering Images

In this chapter, we will cover:

- ▸ Rendering images using content elements
- ▸ Embedding images in RTE
- ▸ Rendering images using TypoScript
- ▸ Rendering links to files using the `<media>` tags
- ▸ Creating a gallery using ce_gallery
- ▸ Rendering metadata from a DAM object

Rendering images using content elements

Content elements offer a variety of ways for editors to include images. We will examine these here. Here is a typical selection menu that editor is presented with:

New content element

Please select the type of page content you wish to create:

Typical page content

- **Regular text element**
  A regular text element with header and bodytext fields.
- **Text with image**
  Any number of images wrapped right around a regular text element.
- **Images only**
  Any number of images aligned in columns and rows with a caption.
- **Bullet list**
  A single bullet list.
- **Table**
  A simple table with up to 8 columns.

Special elements

- **Filelinks**
  Makes a list of files for download.
- **Media**
  Inserts a media element like a Flash animation, audio file or video clip.
- **Sitemap**
  Creates a sitemap of the website.
- **Plain HTML**
  With this element you can insert raw HTML code on the page.
- **Divider**
  This element inserts a visual divider, which is by default a horizontal line.

Form elements

- **Mail form**
  A mail form allowing website users to submit responses.
- **Search form**
  Draws a search form and the searchresult if a search is performed.
- **Login form**
  Login/logout form used to password protect pages allowing only authorised

A great way to start is to assemble pages from the **Regular text element** and the **Text with image** elements.

Getting ready

Make sure **Content (default)** is selected in **Include static**, and the **CSS Styled Content** template is included in the **Include static (from extensions)** field of the template record of the current page or any page above it in the hierarchy (page tree). To verify, go to the **Template** module, select the appropriate page, and click **edit the whole template record**.

How to do it...

1. Create the **Text with image** element.
2. Under the **Text** tab, enter the text you want to appear on the page.

> You can use the **RTE** (**Rich Text Editor**) to apply formatting, or disable it. We will cover RTE in more detail later in this chapter.

3. Under the **Media** tab, select your image settings. If you want to upload the image, use the first field. If you want to use an existing image, use the second field.

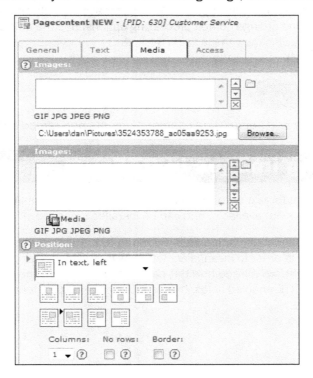

4. Under **Position**, you are able to select where the image will appear in relation to the text.

How it works...

When the page is rendered in the frontend, the images will be placed next to the text you entered, in the position that you specify. The specific look will depend on the template that you are using.

There's more...

An alternative to the **Text with images** is an **Images only** content element. This element gives you similar options, except limits the options to just a display of images. The rest of the options are the same.

You can also resize the image, add caption, `alt` tags for accessibility and search engine optimization, and change default processing options. See the official TYPO3 documentation for details of how these fields work, (`http://typo3.org/documentation/document-library/`).

See also

▸ *Render video and audio using content elements and rgmediaimages extension*

Embedding images in RTE

Rich Text Editor is great for text entry. By default, TYPO3 ships with htmlArea RTE as a system extension. Other editors are available, and can be installed if needed.

Images can be embedded and manipulated within the RTE. This provides one place for content editors to use in order to arrange content how they want it to appear at the frontend of the site. In this recipe, we will see how this can be accomplished. The instructions apply to all forms that have RTE-enabled fields, but we will use the text content element for a simple demonstration.

Getting ready

In the **Extension Manager**, click on htmlArea RTE extension to bring up its options. Make sure that the **Enable images in the RTE [enableImages]** setting is enabled. If you have a recent version of DAM installed (at least 1.1.0), make sure that the **Enable the DAM media browser [enableDAMBrowser]** setting is unchecked. This setting is deprecated, and is there for installations using older versions of DAM.

How to do it...

1. Create a new **Regular text element** content element.

2. In the RTE, click on the icon to insert an image as shown in the following screenshot:

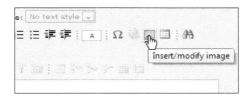

3. Choose a file, and click on the icon to insert it into the **Text** area. You should see the image as it will appear at the frontend of the site.

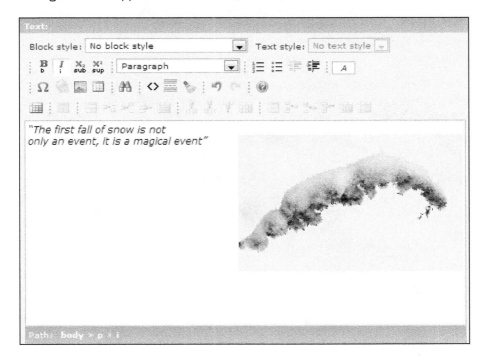

4. Save and preview. The output should appear similar to the following screenshot:

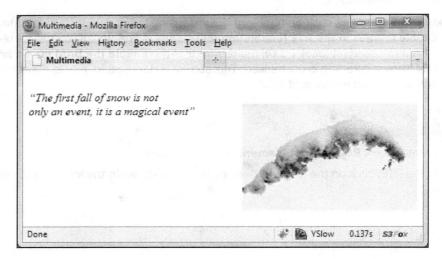

How it works...

When you insert an image through the RTE, the image is copied to `uploads` folder, and included from there. The new file will be resampled and sized down, so, it usually occupies less space and is downloaded faster than the original file. TYPO3 will automatically determine if the original file has changed, and update the file used in the RTE—but you should still be aware of this behaviour.

Furthermore, if you have DAM installed, and you have included an image from DAM, you can see the updated record usage. If you view the record information, you should see the **Content Element** where the image is used:

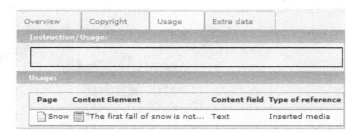

There's more...

There are a few other things you can do in RTE with the images. We will cover:

- ▶ Other modes of inclusion
- ▶ Resizing images
- ▶ Setting maximum dimensions of images
- ▶ Using TinyMCE for embedding images

Other modes of inclusion

When you bring up the **Insert Image** wizard, it has three or more tabs (depending on the extensions you have installed). We've included the image using the default **New Magic Image** tab. Let's see what the other tabs do.

New Plain Image

Plain image inserts the image directly, without creating a copy. If you resize the image in RTE, it will be resized in HTML, but the original file will stay intact. This is different from the resampling behaviour of the Magic Image.

Drag 'n' Drop

Drag 'n' Drop allows you to choose an image in the wizard, and drag it into the RTE. Once you release the mouse button, the image will be inserted into text where your cursor was placed.

Upload

Upload tab appears if you have the DAM extension installed. The tab provides a convenient place to upload images to the server, and include them in the RTE right away, without a need to browse to other modules. This wizard is DAM compatible, so any files that are uploaded will be indexed by the DAM.

Current Image

If you select an image in the RTE, and then click on the **Insert Image** button, you will get the **Insert Image** wizard with a new tab—**Current Image**. Here, you can modify some image properties, or replace the image using the other tabs.

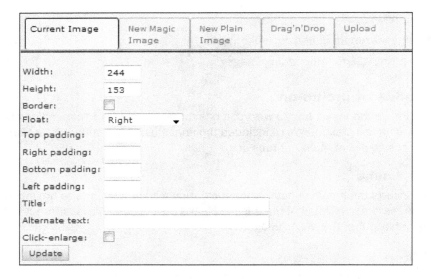

Resizing images

Images can be resized easily within the RTE. To resize an image, click on it, then click and drag one of the corners, or a side to size the image down or up:

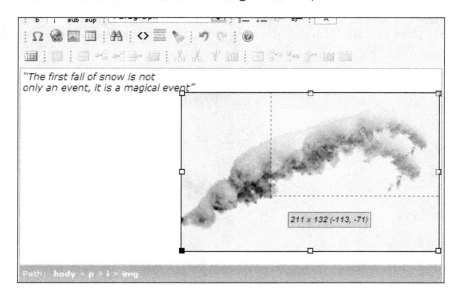

Setting maximum dimensions of images

You can set maximum dimension constraints for all the images added to the RTE. To do so, add the following to `Page TSconfig`:

```
RTE.default.buttons.image.options.magic.maxWidth = 640
RTE.default.buttons.image.options.magic.maxHeight = 480
```

Using TinyMCE for embedding images

Another popular RTE that TYPO3 supports is TinyMCE. It can be enabled by uninstalling `rtehtmlarea` and installing the `tinyrte` extension. Although the interface looks different, the possibilities for image embedding are the same. You can click a button in the toolbar, which brings up a popup window allowing you to select the image you want—as shown in the following screenshots:

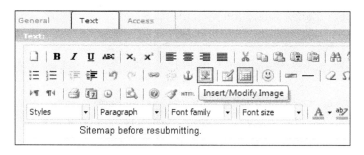

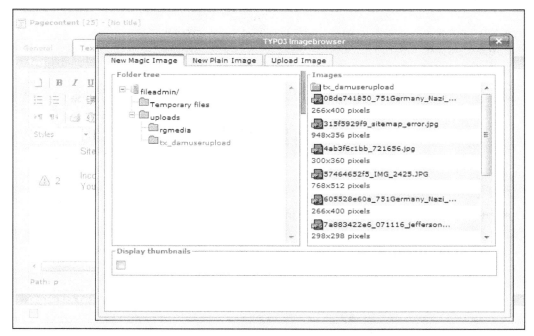

Rendering images using TypoScript

All the content objects available can be created using TypoScript. We will look at the IMAGE content object. Despite its simplicity, there are various situations, in which it is useful. For example, you might need to render an image on several pages, but don't want to include it in the template because it is dynamic. Using TypoScript, you can use conditionals to control which image is rendered, wrap the image in a link, and more. Here, we will first create a simple image, and then see what other options can be given.

How to do it...

1. Modify the template on any page.
2. Add the following code to the setup field, substituting page.12 with the path to the object or marker where you want the image to appear:

```
page.12 = IMAGE
page.12 {
        file = fileadmin/image.jpg
}
```

3. Save, clear cache (if necessary), and preview the page.

How it works...

Content objects take certain parameters as an input, and provide HTML as output. In this case, the input is just a path to a file, but it could be more involved—for examples, see the *There's more...* section.

Check the chapter in TSRef about IMAGE object:
http://typo3.org/documentation/document-library/
references/doc_core_tsref/4.3.0/view/1/7/#id2519243.

There's more...

There are more options besides file that can be passed to the object.

Adding alternative text to images

Alternative text (`alt` tag) can be added to the image using:

```
page.12.altText = Alternative text
```

Likewise, a `title` tag can be added simply by:

```
page.12.titleText = Title text
```

Of course, the values don't have to be hardcoded in, but can come from anywhere in the system by applying `stdWrap` properties.

Wrapping the image in a link

One useful option is having the image as a link. This can be easily done using `stdWrap`:

```
page.12.stdWrap.typolink {
    parameter.data = 123
}
```

where `123` is the page ID that you want to link to.

Executing from an extension

Much like the media object, covered in Chapter 5 the `IMAGE` object can be created from an extension, using the following code:

```
$cObj->cImage($file, $conf);
```

Here, `$file` is the path to the file (which will be resolved by TYPO3, and converted or resized if necessary) and `$conf` is the configuration array for the image object.

See also

  ▸ *Rendering audio and video using media TypoScript object*

Rendering links to files using <media> tags

Imagine, for a second, a dark world of web development without content management systems. You have a simple website with some text and links to files to be downloaded. Now, imagine that you need to move the files into a different folder. You would have to go through each page, and update the links to point to the new location of the file.

In DAM, the physical file is separate from the record describing the file. Thanks to this separation, the pages can link to the DAM record, instead of the physical file. If the file is moved, only the DAM record will need to be updated (which happens automatically if you move the file within DAM modules), and all links will automatically update. We will now explore how the `<media>` HTML tag can be used to take advantage of this feature.

Getting ready

Make sure both DAM and htmlArea RTE extensions are installed. In the **Extension Manager** click on the **DAM extension** to get an overview of **enable configuration**. Make sure that the **media tag** option is enabled.

> **media tag** [mediatag]
> This adds the tag <media> to RTE content processing and frontend rendering. This is needed to create files links using DAM references. Additional page TSconfig may be needed to enable the media tag. See the manual for more information.
> ☑

How to do it...

1. Create a new **Regular text element** on a page.

2. Enter the HTML mode in the RTE:

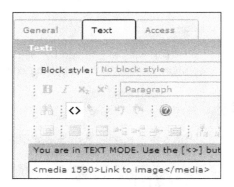

3. Type in `<media 1234>Link text</media>`, replacing `1234` with the UID of the DAM record, and link the text with the text you want to appear inside the link.

You can find the UID of the record in the information panel.

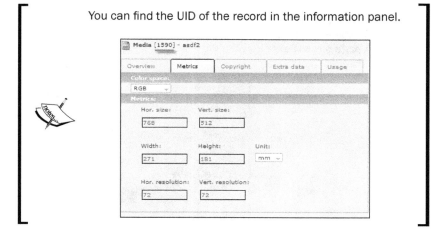

4. Save and preview.

How it works...

The advantage of the `<media>` tag is that instead of linking to a file, you're linking to a DAM record. The record, in turn, points to the physical file—so if you move the files around, all links will be updated automatically.

There's more...

It may be possible that after enabling all the options in the **Extension Manager**, the `<media>` tags are encoded by RTE, and appear in the frontend unparsed. In that case, you need to enter the following options in `Page TSconfig`:

```
// Add txdam_media to RTE processing rules
RTE.default.proc.overruleMode = ts_css,txdam_media

// Use same RTE processing rules in FE
RTE.default.FE.proc.overruleMode = ts_css,txdam_media

// RTE processing rules for bodytext column of tt_content table
RTE.config.tt_content.bodytext.proc.overruleMode = ts_css,txdam_media
RTE.config.tt_content.bodytext.types.text.proc.overruleMode = ts_
css,txdam_media
RTE.config.tt_content.bodytext.types.textpic.proc.overruleMode = ts_
css,txdam_media
```

Accessing Page TSconfig

To access `Page TSconfig`, right-click on a page in the page tree, and choose **Edit page properties**:

Alternatively, you can browse to the page in the **Page** module, and click the **Edit page properties** button either in the module body, or in the **docheader**—the bar across the top of the module housing the control buttons.

From there, the `Page TSConfig` is available under the **Options** tab:

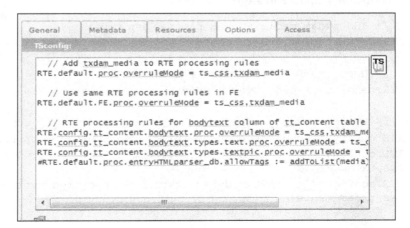

Creating a gallery using ce_gallery

There are multiple galleries available for TYPO3. Each has its own advantages, and an entire book can be dedicated to comparing the various extensions. We will install and configure only one as an example. ce_gallery has an advantage that it is very easy to set up and customize, and relies completely on DAM for content and organization.

Getting ready

Make sure you have the extensions DAM and `dam_catedit` installed. Create a root category, and a few categories under it. Assign a few JPG images to each category. Refer to the Chapter 2 recipe *Setting up a category tree* for more information about categories.

How to do it...

1. Install ce_gallery. Accept database and filesystem changes.
2. In a template record, include the static template **Photogallery (CSS) (ce_gallery)**.
3. Add a **Plugin** content element of type **Photogallery** to a page
4. In the **General** tab, uncheck the **Slimbox (pmkslimbox needed)** checkbox.
5. In the **Categories** tab, select the root category and check the box that says **Recursive**:

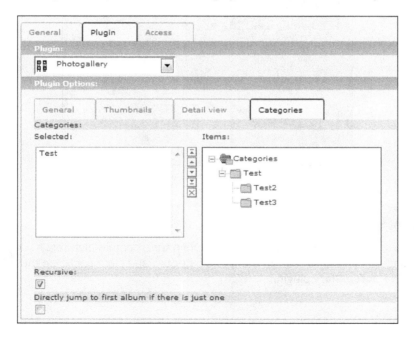

6. Save and preview. The output should appear similar to the following screenshot:

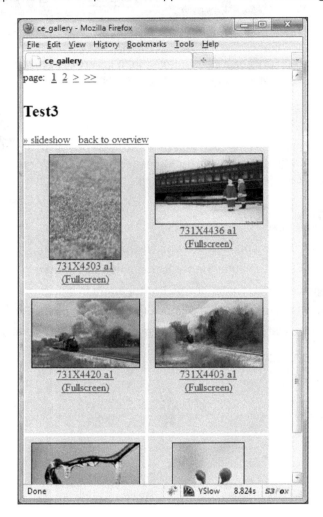

ce_gallery treats DAM categories as albums, which in turn, contain pictures. If you want to add more photos to an album, just assign them to a category, and clear cache on the page where you added the **Photogallery** plugin.

There's more...

In this section, we will see how to use Slimbox for displaying images and utilize batch process while creating a gallery.

Using Slimbox for displaying images

To make use of the Slimbox, you need to install the extension `pmkslimbox`. Once it is installed, include the static template it provides in the page template. When this is done, edit the **Photogallery** content element, and check the **Slimbox (pmkslimbox needed)** checkbox that we had unchecked earlier. Now, instead of linking to another page to display the image, the image will be loaded into the same page using AJAX. For example, this is how your image will look when someone clicks on the thumbnail:

Utilizing batch processing

If you have several photos that you want to assign to a category, you can use DAM's batch operations. Here is what you can do:

Build your selection: You can use the various controls provided by DAM to choose files from multiple folders, of different types, or you can even search the metadata.

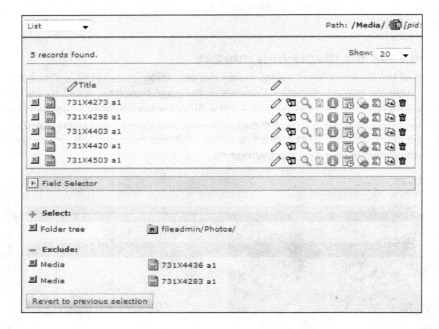

Once you have the selection built, select **Process** from the submodule selector. Under the **Categories** field, select the category you want to add the objects to. If the objects are assigned to other categories, and you don't want to lose that connection, check the box next to the **Categories** field, and the new category will be added to whatever categories the objects are already assigned to. Click **Process** when you're done.

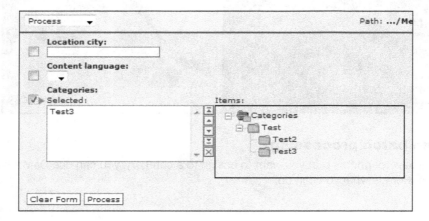

See also

▸ *Setting up a category tree*

Rendering metadata from a DAM object

We'll use some very basic TypoScript and see how metadata stored in DAM records can be rendered on a page, along with the media objects, or even in them. This is commonly used for inserting accessibility tags (`alt` and `title`) into images.

How to do it...

1. Create a **Template** on the page.

2. In the `setup` field, add the following, replacing `page.17` with a path to the object you want to place the content in, and replacing `1234` with the UID for a DAM record, whose caption you would like to display:

```
page.17 = TEXT
page.17.data = DB:tx_dam:1234:caption
```

3. Save and preview.

How it works...

Data property is available wherever `stdWrap` is applied. So, you can display any of the metadata available in the DAM record, almost anywhere. Furthermore, because `stdWrap` properties are recursive, you can apply further processing to the values.

 For more information about `stdWrap`, see the section of TSRef: `http://typo3.org/documentation/document-library/ references/doc_core_tsref/4.3.0/view/1/5/#id2360021`.

In this case, we are using the data property to fetch a record from the database. The syntax for doing so is `DB:table:UID:field`. So, in the example above, we are taking the caption field of record with the UID `1234` from `tx_dam` table.

 Refer to `ext_tables.sql` in the extension directory for a complete database schema.

TypoScript is extremely powerful, so you should read into the details to see what else you can do with it.

There's more...

We can use this method to add a caption to an image, added through TypoScript.

```
page.16 = IMAGE
page.16.altText.data = DB:tx_dam:1585:caption
```

See also

▶   *Rendering images using TypoScript*

5
Rendering Video and Audio

In this chapter, we will cover:

- ▶ Rendering video using media content object
- ▶ Rendering audio using media content object
- ▶ Rendering audio and video using media TypoScript object
- ▶ Rendering audio and video using content elements and rgmediaimages extension
- ▶ Extending the media content object for more rendering options
- ▶ Using custom media player to play video
- ▶ Connecting to Flash Media Server to play video

Rendering video using media content object

One of the new features in TYPO3 4.3 is a new multimedia content object. In this recipe, we will make use of this object to render a video. This method can be used to embed videos in the frontend of the site, allowing visitors to play them from within the page without requiring them to download the file and open it in an external application.

Getting ready

We will render a video in MPG format. Other formats can be rendered just as easily as well, so you can give it a try using the same procedure. Be sure to upload a video into the `fileadmin` folder. See the *There's more...* section to see how to render a video from a URL.

Make sure your template record includes the CSS Styled Content static template, otherwise, you will get an error:

ERROR: Content Element type "media" has no rendering definition!

How to do it...

1. Create a **New content element**, and select **Media** type from the **Special elements** section as shown in the following screenshot:

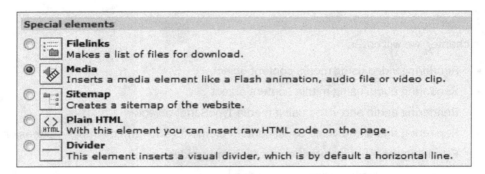

2. Under **relative Path of Media File or URL**, either enter a path to the file, or select the link icon ( ). The following screenshot is seen; browse and select the required file:

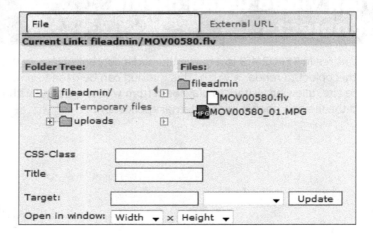

3. Leave the rest of the options as default. Save and preview the page. The output should appear similar to the following screenshot:

There's more...

Quite a few options of the media element can be customized for different outputs.

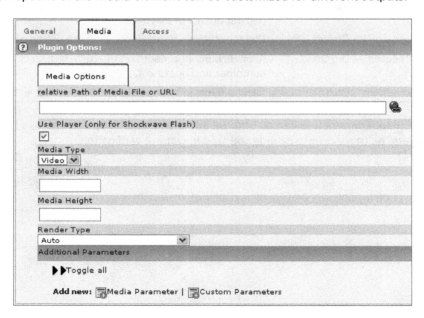

- ▸ **Use Player (only for Shockwave Flash)**: Some videos on the Internet already come with their own embeddable player. If you have entered such a video's URL, you can uncheck the box **Use Player (only for Shockwave Flash)**, otherwise, leave it checked.

- ▸ **Media Type**: Select the type of the media file you want to display.

- ▸ **Media Width/Media Height**: Type in the dimensions of the media object that should render. Dimensions are not constrained by the original file scale.

- ▸ **Render Type**: Select how the file should be rendered. If you're rendering a file, leave this at **Auto**, and TYPO3 will automatically choose the right method based on the file extension. If you're rendering a URL, be sure to set a specific rendering type. Use **Shockwave Flash Browser Plugin** for audio files, and other formats that can be played by an internal SWF player. Use **QuickTime Browser Plugin** for MOV files. Use **HTML Embed Element** for external files, such as YouTube videos, which come with their own player.

The **Additional Parameters** field gives the ability to customize the player by adding more parameters. They will be included in the HTML code for the player. Specific parameters depend on the player you're using. There are two kinds of parameters you can add: **media** and **custom**. Media parameters that can be selected are described below. Each media parameter can be set to **On**, **Off**, or a **Value Entry**, with the value going into the input field below.

Parameter	Value type	Description
Autoplay	On/Off	Start playing the movie/audio when the page is loaded, without waiting for user input.
Loop	On/Off	Restart movie/audio after reaching the end.
Quality	Value Entry	Any value between 0 and 100, 100 corresponding to the highest quality of playback.
Preview Video	On/Off	Display preview of the video file in the media object.
Allow ScriptAccess	On/Off	Allow JavaScript present on the page to access the media container and operate it.
Allow FullScreen	On/Off	Allow the movie to be resized to take up the entire screen.

In addition, custom parameters can be entered into a text field. These can be used to control custom players, as they accept anything you type in without verification.

Embedding external videos

Media object can be used to embed external videos, such as videos hosted on YouTube. Simply enter the video URL in the **relative Path of Media File or URL** field, and uncheck the **Use Player (only for Shockwave Flash)** checkbox.

See also

▸ *Rendering audio using media content object*

▸ *Rendering audio and video using media TypoScript object*

▸ *Extending the media content object for more rendering options*

▸ *Using custom media player to play video*

Rendering audio using media content object

We will now add an audio file to a page, using the same media object. This gives you the ability to embed audio with full controls for playback right into your web page.

How to do it...

1. Create a **New content element** of type **Media.**
2. In the **relative Path of Media File or URL** field, use the wizard to browse for your audio file.
3. Under **Media Type**, select **Audio**.
4. Save and preview. The output should appear similar to the following screenshot:

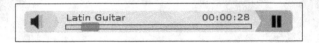

See also

▸ *Rendering video using media content object*

▸ *Rendering audio and video using media TypoScript object*

▸ *Extending the media content object for more rendering options.*

▸ *Using custom media player to play video*

Rendering audio and video using media TypoScript object

Let's now use TypoScript to perform the actions outlined in the recipe *Rendering video using media content object*. This is useful in cases when you want to include an object on several pages, and still be administrated in one place, or if the position in the template is strange, and content editors are unable to get to it using the **Page** module.

Getting ready

We will assume that you have the template for the site set up, and you have a marker in the template that you want to replace.

How to do it...

1. Edit the **Template** record.

2. Add the following lines to the `setup` field (modifying the path to the marker and path to the file):

   ```
   page.10.marks.VIDEO < tt_content.media.20
   page.10.marks.VIDEO.file = fileadmin/movie.mpg
   page.10.marks.VIDEO.renderType = qt
   ```

3. Clear all cache and preview the page. The output should appear similar to the following screenshot:

How it works...

`tt_content.media.20` is a TypoScript array that contains the definition of a MEDIA type object. The first line copies the configuration into the VIDEO marker. The subsequent lines modify the default configuration, and customize it—the same way a form does.

There's more...

All other options of the media object can be controlled through TypoScript. Look in the TypoScript Object Browser for all options and settings:

```
[20] = MEDIA
  [flexParams]
  [alternativeContent] = TEXT
  [type] = video
  [renderType] = auto
  [allowEmptyUrl] = 0
  [fileExtHandler]
  [mimeConf]
    [swfobject] = SWFOBJECT
      [file] =
      [width] =
      [height] =
      [flexParams]
      [alternativeContent]
      [layout] = ###SWFOBJECT###
      [video]
        [player] = typo3/contrib/flashmedia/flvplayer...
        [defaultWidth] = 600
        [defaultHeight] = 400
        [default]
        [mapping]
      [audio]
      [stdWrap]
    [qtobject] = QTOBJECT
  [stdWrap]
```

Rendering audio and video using content elements and rgmediaimages extension

Various extensions modify and build upon default TYPO3 behavior (as we have seen already). In this recipe, we will make use of the rgmediaimages extension to add videos to the Text with image content element. This is a classic example of extending default TYPO3 behavior and adding more functionality to the system.

Getting ready

We assume you have already installed the rgmediaimages extension. If not, use the information in the Chapter 1 recipe *Installing needed extensions* to install it now.

How to do it...

1. In the **Template** module, modify the template for the page (click **edit the whole template record**).

2. In the **Includes** tab, under the **Include static (from extensions)** field, select the **Media files & images (rgmediaimages)** template, as shown in the following screenshot, and save.

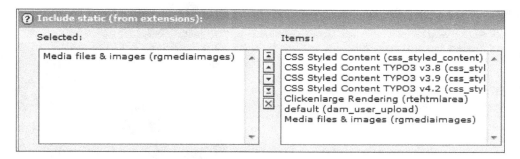

3. In the **Page** module, create a new **Text with image** content element on the page.

4. Under the **Text** tab, enter any text you would like.

5. Under the **Media** tab, select the files you would like to include. The selection is no longer limited to just images, so you can select movies and audio files.

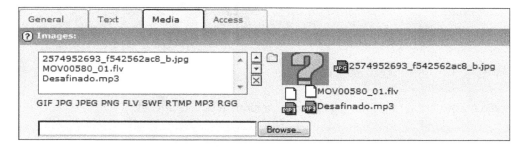

6. Enter maximum width and height values to restrict the content. These values are required in some circumstances—see the extension manual for more information.

7. Save and preview. The output should appear similar to the following screenshot:

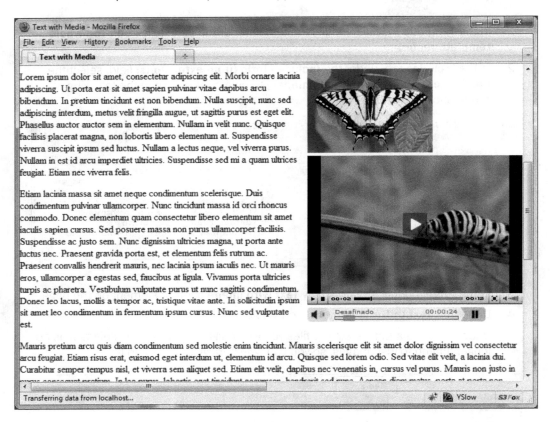

There's more...

rgmediaimages has a few other configuration options that you can set.

Customizing FLV and MP3 output

An individual item's display can be customized within the object. Scroll down to **Alternative Text** field, and type in the options that will be sent to the JW FLV player. Each line corresponds to each file, and settings are separated by commas as shown in the following screenshot:

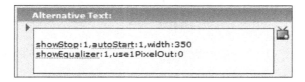

Alternatively, you can click on the icon to the right to launch the wizard, which will give you a form for customization as shown in the following screenshot.

```
WIZARD FOR THE EXTENSION RGMEDIAIMAGES

 #1: 2574952693_f542562ac8_b.jpg
     Default
   File                        [                    ]


 #2: MOV00580_01.flv
     Default
   File                        [                    ]

     The colors

     Display appearance

     Controlbar appearance
   Show Navigation      true  ▾
   Show Stop            true  ▾
   Show Digits          true  ▾
   Show Download        false ▾

     Playback behaviour


 #3: Desafinado.mp3
     Default
   File                        [                    ]

     The colors

     Display appearance
```

You can also modify the parameters that are used throughout the site, or within a certain section of the page tree. These are constants, and can be modified in the **Constant Editor** under the **Template** module as shown in the following screenshot:

For more information, as well as a complete reference to the plugin settings, refer to the extension manual.

Embedding YouTube videos

rgmediaimages can be used to embed external videos, such as videos from YouTube. Here are the steps to do it:

1. Upload dummy.rgg file from extension's resource folder (rgmediaimages/res/ dummy.rgg) into any folder under fileadmin.

 If you can't find the file, create an empty text document, and rename it dummy.rgg.

2. Select the file in the **Images** field of the **Text with images** content element.

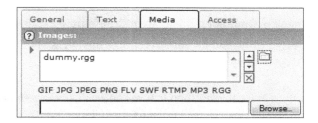

3. Under **Alternative Text** field, enter `file:` followed by the URL of the clip. For example: `file:http://www.youtube.com/watch?v=a1Y73sPHKxw`.

 Alternatively, you can enter the information through the wizard, launched by clicking on the icon to the right of the **Alternative Text** field.

4. Save and preview.

See also

▸ *Installing needed extensions*

Extending the media content object for more rendering options

While the media object is really powerful, occasionally, you may need a specialized method for rendering files. Luckily, the object is extensible. In this recipe, we will create a new plugin for rendering audio files.

Getting ready

As we will be creating a new extension, make sure Kickstarter is installed.

We will be using SoundManager 2 JavaScript code as an example. You can integrate any other audio or video plugin into the media object. To learn more about SoundManager 2, visit `http://www.schillmania.com/projects/soundmanager2/`.

How to do it...

1. Go to the **Extension Manager** module, then **Create new Extension**.

2. Enter your extension key, and be sure to register the key, so no one else uses it. For this extension, you can enter `soundmanager2`.

 If you're creating an extension that will only be used in your installation, and will not be released to **TYPO3 Extension Repository** (**TER**), use a `user_` prefix in the extension key.

3. Click on the plus icon (**+**) next to the **General info** to edit the basic required information about the extension.

4. Click **View result**, and write the output to the default location.

5. Download the latest release of SoundManager2 from the site: `http://www.schillmania.com/projects/soundmanager2/`.

 At the time this book was written, the latest version was 2.95a.20090717. This is likely to change. Be sure to review how SoundManager works, and verify that the plugin code issues correct calls to its API.

6. Edit `ext_emconf.php`, add the following element in the `depends` array:

   ```
   'typo3' => '4.3.0-0.0.0',
   ```

7. Create `ext_localconf.php` file and add the following:

   ```php
   <?php
   if (!defined ('TYPO3_MODE')) {
           die ('Access denied.');
   }


   // Register Hooks
   $TYPO3_CONF_VARS['SC_OPTIONS']['tslib/hooks/class.tx_cms_
   mediaitems.php']['customMediaRenderTypes'][$_EXTKEY] = 'EXT:' .
   $_EXTKEY . '/class.tx_soundmanager2.php:tx_soundmanager2';
   $TYPO3_CONF_VARS['SC_OPTIONS']['tslib/hooks/class.tx_cms_
   mediaitems.php']['customMediaRender'][$_EXTKEY] = 'EXT:' . $_
   EXTKEY . '/class.tx_soundmanager2.php:tx_soundmanager2';
   ?>
   ```

8. Create `class.tx_soundmanager2.php` with the content from the code pack available with the book.

How it works...

We will now go through all the files, and see how they make our extension run.

ext_localconf.php

This file is loaded when TYPO3 is initializing, and it's a perfect spot to place all our hook definitions.

```
// Register Hooks
$TYPO3_CONF_VARS['SC_OPTIONS']['tslib/hooks/class.tx_cms_mediaitems.
php']['customMediaRenderTypes'][$_EXTKEY] = 'EXT:' . $_EXTKEY . '/
class.tx_soundmanager2.php:tx_soundmanager2';
$TYPO3_CONF_VARS['SC_OPTIONS']['tslib/hooks/class.tx_cms_mediaitems.
php']['customMediaRender'][$_EXTKEY] = 'EXT:' . $_EXTKEY . '/class.
tx_soundmanager2.php:tx_soundmanager2';
```

$TYPO3_CONF_VARS['SC_OPTIONS']['tslib/hooks/class.tx_cms_mediaitems.
php']['customMediaRenderTypes'] holds an array of class references. Any class referenced would implement the function customMediaRenderTypes, which is called by the media content element flexform when the record is being created or edited. Same is true for the $TYPO3_CONF_VARS['SC_OPTIONS']['tslib/hooks/class.tx_cms_
mediaitems.php']['customMediaRender'] array, which holds the list of classes implementing the customMediaRender function. We implement these functions in the same class tx_soundmanager2, stored in class.tx_soundmanager2.php.

class. tx_soundmanager2.php

Let's look at the detailed implementation of the two functions we just mentioned.

customMediaRenderTypes()

This function is passed two parameters—$params and $conf.
$conf contains the full TypoScript configuration of the media object—we will not need it at this time. $params contains an array of render types—including the default ones.
We add an item to the list, with the name 'SoundManager 2' and ID 'soundmanager2'.

```
$params['items'][] = array(
    0 => 'SoundManager 2',
    1 => 'soundmanager2'
);
```

Because both arrays are passed by reference, we don't need to return anything from the function. But be careful, if you inadvertently change any of the values, the media object might fail to work as desired.

customMediaRender()

This function is called when the media content object is rendered on the frontend. It will be called for all media content objects displayed on an installation where the extension is installed, so the first thing that the function does is verifies that the render type selected matches the render type it's designed to handle:

```
if ($renderType == 'soundmanager2') {
    ...
}
```

 Alternatively, the customMediaRender function can modify the default behavior of other render types; however, this is not recommended, as it can cause interference and unpredictable results.

If render type is indeed selected as desired, we proceed to create the HTML code that will be displayed on the page.

First, we create some parameters:

```
// Unique id for a sound.
$soundID = t3lib_div::shortMD5($conf['file'], 6);
// Check if volume is defined - if not - define it.
$conf['soundmanager2']['volume'] =
    $conf['soundmanager2']['volume'] ?
    $conf['soundmanager2']['volume'] : '50';
```

The second line indicates that the default starting volume could be set in TypoScript using:

```
tt_content.media.20.soundmanager2.volume = 80;
```

Next, we include the soundmanager 2 JavaScript library. As this library needs to be included in the <head> section of HTML, we use the **TSFE** additionalHeaderData to place it there—if it wasn't placed there by another media object already:

```
$GLOBALS['TSFE']->additionalHeaderData['tx_soundmanager2'] =
'<script type="text/javascript" src="'
    . $scriptPath . '"></script>' . "\n";
```

The script path depends on another setting:

```
tt_content.media.20.soundmanager2.minify = 1;
```

If set, a compressed version of the library is included—making it download and run faster in the browser, but removing some of the debugging options we would find useful during development. We decide on which script to include with the following:

```
if ($conf['soundmanager.']['minify']) {
    $scriptPath = $GLOBALS['TSFE']->tmpl->
      getFileName('EXT:soundmanager2/res/script/
        soundmanager2-nodebug-jsmin.js');
} else {
    $scriptPath = $GLOBALS['TSFE']->tmpl->
      getFileName('EXT:soundmanager2/res/script/soundmanager2.js');
}
```

Finally, we create the JavaScript code to create a `Sound` object, and play it upon page load. We then wrap it in standard JavaScript tags, and return it to the media content object, which in turn includes it into the page.

```
$contentJS .= "soundManager.onload = function() {
    // SM2 is ready to go!
    var sound_" . $soundID . " = soundManager.createSound({
        id: 's" . $soundID . "',
        url: '" . $conf['file'] . "',
        volume: " . $conf['soundmanager2']['volume'] . "
    });
}\n";

$GLOBALS['TSFE']->additionalHeaderData['tx_soundmanager2'] .=
    t3lib_div::wrapJS($contentJS);
$content = 'sound_" . $soundID . ".play();';

return t3lib_div::wrapJS($content);
```

See SoundManager 2 documentation for more information on how the JavaScript code works, as well as more options that can be used to manipulate it.

See also

▶ *Rendering audio using media content object*

Using custom media player to play video

Much like we did with audio, we will now create an extension to embed FLV player and render a custom video. You can use the same approach to embed any other custom video player to play your movies.

 For more information about FLV player, visit `http://flvplayer.com/`.

Getting ready

Make sure you have read and understood *Extending the media content object for more rendering options* recipe covered earlier. This recipe follows the same steps, using slightly different code. You should have created an extension skeleton in Kickstarter.

How to do it...

1. Create `ext_localconf.php` if it doesn't exist, and add the following content:

```php
<?php
if (!defined ('TYPO3_MODE')) {
    die ('Access denied.');
}

// Register Hooks
$TYPO3_CONF_VARS['SC_OPTIONS']['tslib/hooks/class.tx_cms_
mediaitems.php']['customMediaRenderTypes'][$_EXTKEY] = 'EXT:' .
$_EXTKEY . '/class.tx_webflvplayer.php:tx_webflvplayer';
$TYPO3_CONF_VARS['SC_OPTIONS']['tslib/hooks/class.tx_cms_
mediaitems.php']['customMediaRender'][$_EXTKEY] = 'EXT:' . $_
EXTKEY . '/class.tx_webflvplayer.php:tx_webflvplayer';
$TYPO3_CONF_VARS['SC_OPTIONS']['tslib/hooks/class.tx_cms_
mediaitems.php']['customMediaParams'][$_EXTKEY] = 'EXT:' . $_
EXTKEY . '/class.tx_webflvplayer.php:tx_webflvplayer';
?>
```

2. Copy the file `class.tx_webflvplayer.php` from the code pack downloaded from the book's site.

3. Create a new **Media** element. Enter a URL to an FLV file you want to display.

FLV player requires a URL to be entered.

4. Check the **Use Player** checkbox.

5. Under **Render Type**, you should see **FLV Player**. Select it.

6. If you add a new media parameter, you should see a new option **Background color (in hexadecimal)**, which you can select, and enter the value in the **Value** input field:

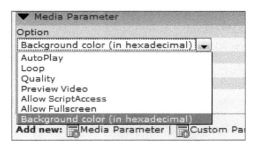

7. Save and preview. You should see a player like this on the page:

Let's take a look at the extension, and dissect what each function does.

ext_localconf.php

This file contains our hook registers. References to the `tx_webflvplayer` class are added to all three hooks that the media object provides.

class.tx_webflvplayer.php

This is where the magic happens, so let's look at it in detail, function by function.

customMediaRenderTypes()

This function adds FLV player to the **Render Type** select box.

```
$params['items'][] = array(
    0 => 'FLV Player',
    1 => 'web_flvplayer'
);
```

customMediaParams()

This function adds the **Background color** option into the **Media Parameter** select box:

```
$params['items'][] = array(
    0 => 'Background color (in hexadecimal)',
    1 => 'bgColor'
);
```

 Any options added in this function will be available in the **Media Parameter** select box regardless of the selected render type.

customMediaRender()

This is the main function of our class. It will be executed for every media content element, so we first need to verify that the **Render Type** has been selected as **FLV Player**:

```
if ($renderType == 'web_flvplayer') {
```

`web_flvplayer` is the value we've given to the choice in the `customMediaRenderTypes()` function. Next, we set some variables—options controlling the player's appearance and functionality. We set some defaults in case the parameters were not set in the content element configuration.

The next order of business is to go through the media parameters and custom parameters, and change the default values based on whether the options have been set:

```php
if (is_array($conf['parameter.']['mmMediaOptions']
    ['mmMediaOptionsContainer'])) {
    foreach ($conf['parameter.']['mmMediaOptions']
        ['mmMediaOptionsContainer'] as $mediaOption) {
        switch ($mediaOption['mmParamName']) {
            case 'allowFullScreen':
                $allowFullScreen = ($mediaOption['mmParamSet'] == 1)
                    ? 'true' : 'false';
                break;
            case 'allowScriptAccess':
                $allowScriptAccess =
                        ($mediaOption['mmParamSet'] == 1) ?
                    $mediaOption['mmParamValue'] : 'false';
                break;
            case 'quality':
                $quality = $mediaOption['mmParamValue'];
                break;
            case 'bgColor':
                $bgColor = $mediaOption['mmParamValue'];
        }
    }
}
```

Media parameters are stored in the `$conf['parameter.']['mmMediaOptions']` `['mmMediaOptionsContainer']` array. Each element is in turn an array that has the parameter name (`mmParamName`), value (`mmParamValue`), and the value of the on/off switch (`mmParamSet`). What we do with these values is completely upto the extensions—so, we use a switch statement to process every element and set our variables, to which we assigned their default values previously.

Next, we parse out the custom parameters. As these are entered into a text field, presumably they're just HTML tags, so we compile them into a string:

```php
if (is_array($conf['parameter.']['mmMediaOptions']
    ['mmMediaCustomParameterContainer'])) {
    foreach ($conf['parameter.']['mmMediaOptions']
        ['mmMediaCustomParameterContainer'] as $mediaOption) {
        $customParameters .= $mediaOption['mmParamCustomEntry'] . "\n";
    }
}
```

Finally, we create the player HTML code, using `object` and `param` HTML tags, and substituting our variables where appropriate. We then return the HTML content.

There's more...

There are a few other things we can do to improve the extension.

Utilizing templates

We can take the HTML code completely out of this extension, placing it into a template file, which could be changed by the user. Let's do that:

1. Create a new folder `res`, in it an HTML file `flv_player.html`, with the following content:

    ```
    <object classid="clsid:d27cdb6e-ae6d-11cf-96b8-444553540000"
    codebase="http://download.macromedia.com/pub/shockwave/cabs/
    flash/swflash.cab#version=9,0,0,0" width="640" height="375"
    id="FlvPlayer" align="middle">
    <param name="allowScriptAccess" value="###ALLOW_SCRIPT_ACCESS###"
    />
    <param name="allowFullScreen" value="###ALLOW_FULL_SCREEN###" />
    <param name="movie" value="http://flvplayer.com/free-flv-player/
    FlvPlayer.swf" />
    <param name="quality" value="###QUALITY###" />
    <param name="bgcolor" value="###BGCOLOR###" />
    ###CUSTOM_PARAMETERS###<param name="FlashVars" value="flvpFolderLo
    cation=http://flvplayer.com/free-flv-player/flvplayer/&flvpVideoSo
    urce=###FILE###&flvpWidth=###WIDTH###&flvpHeight=###HEIGHT###&flvp
    InitVolume=50&flvpTurnOnCorners=true&flvpBgColor=###BGCOLOR###" />
    <embed src="http://flvplayer.com/free-flv-player/FlvPlayer.
    swf" flashvars="flvpFolderLocation=http://flvplayer.com/free-
    flv-player/flvplayer/&flvpVideoSource=###FILE###&flvpWidth=###
    WIDTH###&flvpHeight=###HEIGHT###&flvpInitVolume=50&flvpTurnOnC
    orners=true&flvpBgColor=###BGCOLOR###" quality="###QUALITY###"
    bgcolor="###BGCOLOR###" width="###WIDTH###" height="###HEIGHT###"
    name="FlvPlayer" align="middle" allowScriptAccess="###ALLOW_
    SCRIPT_ACCESS###" allowFullScreen="###ALLOW_FULL_SCREEN###"
    type="application/x-shockwave-flash" pluginspage="http://www.
    adobe.com/go/getflashplayer" />
    ###ALTERNATIVE_CONTENT###
    </object>
    ```

2. Change the `customMediaRender()` function in `class.tx_webflvplayer.php` to the following:

    ```
    function customMediaRender($renderType, $conf) {
        if ($renderType == 'web_flvplayer') {
            // Initialize cObject
            $cObj = t3lib_div::makeInstance('tslib_cObj');

            // Set some parameters
    ```

```php
        $markers['###FILE###'] = $conf['file'];
        $markers['###WIDTH###'] = isset($conf['width']) ?
          $conf['width'] : 640;
        $markers['###HEIGHT###'] = isset($conf['height']) ?
          $conf['height'] : 480;

        $markers['###ALLOW_FULL_SCREEN###'] = 'true';
        $markers['###ALLOW_SCRIPT_ACCESS###'] = 'sameDomain';
        $markers['###QUALITY###'] = 'high';
        $markers['###BGCOLOR###'] = 'FFFFFF';
        $markers['###CUSTOM_PARAMETERS###'] = '';
        $markers['###ALTERNATIVE_CONTENT###'] = $cObj->stdWrap
          ($conf['alternativeContent'],
            $conf['alternativeContent.']);

        // Go through the parameters
        if (is_array($conf['parameter.']['mmMediaOptions']
          ['mmMediaOptionsContainer'])) {
            foreach ($conf['parameter.']['mmMediaOptions']
              ['mmMediaOptionsContainer'] as $mediaOption) {
                switch ($mediaOption['mmParamName']) {
                    case 'allowFullScreen':

$markers['###ALLOW_FULL_SCREEN###'] =
  ($mediaOption['mmParamSet'] == 1) ? 'true' : 'false';
                    break;
                    case 'allowScriptAccess':

$markers['###ALLOW_SCRIPT_ACCESS###'] =
        ($mediaOption['mmParamSet'] == 1) ?
          $mediaOption['mmParamValue'] : 'false';
                    break;
                    case 'quality':

$markers['###QUALITY###'] = $mediaOption['mmParamValue'];
                    break;
                    case 'bgColor':

$markers['###BGCOLOR###'] = $mediaOption['mmParamValue'];
            }
          }
        }
        if (is_array($conf['parameter.']['mmMediaOptions']
['mmMediaCustomParameterContainer'])) {
```

```
                    foreach ($conf['parameter.']['mmMediaOptions']
                        ['mmMediaCustomParameterContainer'] as $mediaOption)
    {
        $markers['###CUSTOM_PARAMETERS###'] .= $mediaOption
          ['mmParamCustomEntry'] . "\n";
                }
            }

            $templateFile = isset($conf['web_flvplayer']) ?
                $conf['web_flvplayer'] : t3lib_extMgm::extPath
                  ('web_flvplayer') . 'res/flv_player.html';
            $template = $cObj->fileResource($templateFile);

            // Gather the HTML content for the player
            $content = $cObj->substituteMarkerArray
              ($template, $markers);
            return $content;
        }
    }
```

Download the extension `web_flvplayer2` from the code pack, and compare it to your result.

What did we change? Now, all the parameters are compiled into an array, and the keys of the array are markers. The template file now has markers that can be replaced by the values from the array. This way we effectively separated all presentation (HTML code) from the business logic (PHP code).

Furthermore, we have made our extension more configurable. Now, to change the template, either for the whole site, or for part of the page tree, a user would need to add the following line to the `setup` field of the template record:

```
tt_content.media.20.web_flvplayer = /path/to/template.html
```

The template file can be stored in `fileadmin`, and can be modified by backend users without admin access.

Commercial players

We've used the free player for demonstration. Commercial player can be used as well, with some slight modifications. We'll leave it to the reader to figure out the changes that need to be made.

See also

 ▸ *Rendering video using media content object*
 ▸ *Extending the media content object for more rendering options*

Connecting to Flash Media Server to play video

Flash Media Server (**FMS**) is an amazing piece of software from Adobe that provides streaming and interactivity to the Web. Audio and video could be streamed in different resolutions, with limited buffering. Furthermore, Flash Media Server allows to stream live video!

We will not dig into the internal configuration of Flash Media Server, as that would require a book on its own. All the control elements for the client is packaged into a SWF file that can be deployed to the Web. In this recipe, we will look at how the code can be embedded in TYPO3 to communicate with a Flash Media Server.

How to do it...

1. Create an HTML element on the page.
2. Add the following code (you can copy it from the introductory page of the FMS installation). Replace the URLs to point to your Flash Media Server.

```
<object width='640' height='377' id='videoPlayer'
name='videoPlayer' type='application/x-shockwave-flash'
classid='clsid:d27cdb6e-ae6d-11cf-96b8-444553540000' ><param
name='movie' value='http://localhost/swfs/videoPlayer.swf' />
<param name='quality' value='high' /> <param name='bgcolor'
value='#000000' /> <param name='allowfullscreen' value='true' />
<param name='flashvars' value= '&videoWidth=0&videoHeight=0&dsC
ontrol=manual&dsSensitivity=100&serverURL=http://localhost/vod/
sample2_1000kbps.f4v&DS_Status=true&streamType=vod&autoStart=true
&videoWidth=0&videoHeight=0&dsControl=manual&dsSensitivity=100&se
rverURL=dynamicStream.smil&DS_Status=true&streamType=vod&autoStart
=true&videoWidth=0&videoHeight=0&dsControl=manual&dsSensitivity=10
0&serverURL=http://localhost/vod/sample2_1000kbps.f4v&DS_Status=tr
ue&streamType=vod&autoStart=true&videoWidth=0&videoHeight=0&dsCont
rol=manual&dsSensitivity=100&serverURL=dynamicStream.smil&DS_Statu
s=true&streamType=vod&autoStart=true&videoWidth=0&videoHeight=0&d
sControl=manual&dsSensitivity=100&serverURL=http://localhost/vod/
sample2_1000kbps.f4v&DS_Status=true&streamType=vod&autoStart=true
'/><embed src='http://localhost/swfs/videoPlayer.swf' width='640'
height='377' id='videoPlayer' quality='high' bgcolor='#000000'
name='videoPlayer' allowfullscreen='true' pluginspage='http://www.
adobe.com/go/getflashplayer'    flashvars='&videoWidth=0&videoHeigh
t=0&dsControl=manual&dsSensitivity=100&serverURL=http://localhost/
vod/sample2_1000kbps.f4v&DS_Status=true&streamType=vod&autoStart=t
rue&videoWidth=0&videoHeight=0&dsControl=manual&dsSensitivity=100&
serverURL=dynamicStream.smil&DS_Status=true&streamType=vod&autoSta
rt=true&videoWidth=0&videoHeight=0&dsControl=manual&dsSensitivity=
100&serverURL=http://localhost/vod/sample2_1000kbps.f4v&DS_Status=
true&streamType=vod&autoStart=true&videoWidth=0&videoHeight=0&dsCo
```

```
ntrol=manual&dsSensitivity=100&serverURL=dynamicStream.smil&DS_Sta
tus=true&streamType=vod&autoStart=true&videoWidth=0&videoHeight=0&
dsControl=manual&dsSensitivity=100&serverURL=http://localhost/vod/
sample2_1000kbps.f4v&DS_Status=true&streamType=vod&autoStart=true'
type='application/x-shockwave-flash'> </embed></object>
```

You can copy this code from the introductory page of the FMS installation.

3. Save and preview, the output can be seen in the the following screenshot:

How it works...

The HTML element simply includes the HTML code on the page. In this case, we're including an SWF movie from the FMS server. All the work of communicating with the FMS is done by the Flash SFW we have included.

There's more...

You can include the same code in other places besides the HTML content element.

Embedding Flash in RTE

Flash movies, including those driven by Flash Media Server can be embedded in Rich Text Editor as well. To be able to do that, you need to first add the `object`, `embed`, and `param` HTML tags to the list of tags the RTE is allowed to preserve—otherwise, they will be stripped out. Add this to `Page TSconfig`:

```
RTE.default.proc.allowTags := addToList(object,param,embed)
RTE.default.proc.entryHTMLparser_db.allowTags :=
addToList(object,param,embed)
```

Then, enter RTE's HTML mode, and paste the same HTML code in:

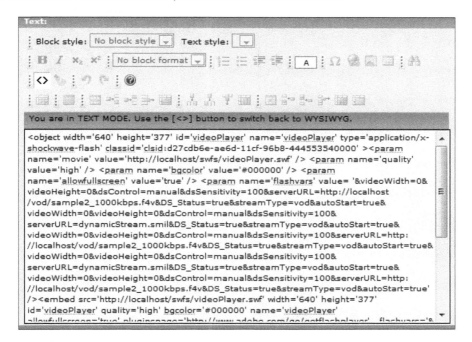

See also

▸ *Embedding images in RTE*

▸ *Rendering video using the media content object*

6

Connecting to External APIs

In this chapter, we will cover:

- ▶ Getting files from Amazon S3
- ▶ Uploading files to S3
- ▶ Creating a bucket in S3
- ▶ Uploading DAM files to S3
- ▶ Getting recent Flickr photos
- ▶ Uploading files to Flickr
- ▶ Uploading DAM files to Flickr
- ▶ Reading a list of movies from the YouTube API
- ▶ Authenticating requests to the YouTube API
- ▶ Showing a video list with a frontend plugin

Introduction

One of the great features of the Web 2.0 world is the connectivity. Most online services and applications provide **Application Programming Interfaces** (**API**) that expose their data and functionality. As an application developer, you have access to these APIs, and can utilize them to provide functionality that you would otherwise have a tough time implementing. This chapter covers general approaches to working with public APIs, using Amazon S3, Flickr, and YouTube as examples.

Getting files from Amazon S3

Amazon S3 is the distributed file system that can be used over the Web. It's nearly limitless in terms of storage capacity, it's cheap, and you pay only for what you use. S3 has recently become very popular for these reasons.

Getting ready

Before we get started, you need to understand some of the basic features of S3, in order to create an application that makes the best use of the system. There are two resources under S3—buckets and objects. **Objects** are files, while buckets hold collections of objects. **Buckets** can be public or private, with **Access Control Lists** (**ACLs**) for finer permissions control. Objects can be accessed through the browser by URIs. Objects can also have complex names, making up for the lack of folders.

 To learn more about S3 and sign up for the account, go to `http://aws.amazon.com/`.

We will be using the Amazon S3 PHP class for all our interfacing with the S3 service. You can download it from `http://code.google.com/p/amazon-s3-php-class/`.

Feel free to read through example files to see how the file should be used, but the only file we really need is `S3.php`.

The class requires **cURL** to be installed. Here is how you can check if it is installed, and working, on your TYPO3 site:

1. Go to **Admin tools | Install** module.

 If you get an error stating that the **Install Tool is locked**, go to **User tools | User setting**, and click **Create Install Tool Enable File**. See *Resolving missing ENABLE_INSTALL_TOOL file error* tip in *Creating scalable architecture* recipe in Chapter 1 for more information.

2. Chose option **phpinfo()**.
3. Look for **cURL support**—it should be enabled.

curl	
cURL support	enabled
cURL Information	libcurl/7.16.0 OpenSSL/0.9.8g zlib/1.2.3

4. If not, you can install it using APT on a Debian System:

```
Shell> apt-get install php5-curl
```

The following steps assume you already have an extension ready, and are adding S3 support into the existing code. Thus, we will not get into details of the steps needed to create a new extension. Assuming everything is ready, you can proceed to listing the files.

How to do it...

1. In a PHP file, add the following before the declaration of the class:

```
require_once('S3.php');
```

2. Verify that the path to S3.php is correct, and if not, modify it to point to the correct location.

3. In a function where you would like to get the list of files, add the following code:

```
$s3 = new S3('access code', 'secret code');
$buckets = $s3->listBuckets();
foreach ($buckets as $bucketName) {
    if (($contents = $s3->getBucket($bucketName)) !== false) {
        foreach ($contents as $objectName => $object) {
            $objects[$bucketName . '/' . $objectName] = $object;
            $objects[$bucketName . '/' . $objectName]['bucket'] =
                $bucketName;
        }
    }
}
```

4. Replace 'access code' with your actual access code—you can find this information in Amazon—under your **Account | Security Credentials**. Do the same for the string 'secret code'.

5. To print the results, use the following code:

```
foreach ($objects as $object) {
    print_r($object);
}
```

6. It will result in an output similar to:

```
Array
(
    [name] => S3.php
    [time] => 1253554887
    [size] => 49961
    [hash] => 2f3d98f42e66f6db6e19e9cac3f65cbc
    [bucket] => s3test4ab7b8fcd484e
)
```

How it works...

All the hard work is being done by the S3 class, so the first thing we did was include it, and then instantiate the object:

```
$s3 = new S3('access code', 'secret code');
```

> If you get a certificate error, there is a problem in communicating to S3 via secure HTTP. Change the instantiation line to:
>
> ```
> $s3 = new S3('access code', 'secret code', FALSE);
> ```
>
> where the last parameter tells S3 class not to use the HTTPS protocol.

Next, we listed all the buckets we have in S3:

```
$buckets = $s3->listBuckets();
```

this line returns an array of bucket names. If you only want to list files in a particular bucket, use the name of the bucket instead of a loop:

```
$bucketName = 'MyTestBucket';
if (($contents = $s3->getBucket($bucketName)) !== false) {
    foreach ($contents as $objectName => $object) {
        $objects[$bucketName . '/' . $objectName] = $object;
        $objects[$bucketName . '/' . $objectName]['bucket'] =
            $bucketName;
    }
}
```

Next, we get the contents of each bucket. Sometimes, S3 may not return anything—either because the bucket is inaccessible due to security policy, or it was just created, and hasn't replicated to all nodes yet.

If we do have content in the bucket, the list of files is placed in the $contents variable. We loop over the variable, and reassign it to a different array, along with the bucket name. At the end, $objects contains a full listing of files, along with their size in bytes, time uploaded as a UNIX timestamp, and hash of the file content.

There's more...

Of course, there are a lot more options for listing objects, which become necessary in large object lists.

Searching for objects

If you want to only see objects whose name starts with a certain string, you can pass the second parameter to the function:

```
$contents = $s3->getBucket($bucketName, 'MyVideos/2009');
```

 A common workaround that deals with the absence of categories in S3 is to create object names that reflect their position in the hierarchy. For example:

`MyVideos/2009/January/24/Mountain.avi.`

Then, objects in certain pseudo directories can be found using the prefix as shown above.

Finding common prefixes

You can find out what the common prefixes among the files are to aid you in searching.

```
$contents = $s3->getBucket($bucketName, NULL, NULL, NULL, '/', TRUE);
```

Working with large object lists

If you have a large set of objects stored in S3, the listing operation may take a lot of time. It's possible to limit the number of results returned using markers and limits.

```
$contents = $s3->getBucket($bucketName, NULL, 'S3.php', 25);
```

The marker is the file after which the results should start.

See also

- ▶ *Uploading files to S3*
- ▶ *Creating a bucket in S3*
- ▶ *Uploading DAM files to S3*
- ▶ *Creating a scalable architecture*

Uploading files to S3

If you just set up your S3 account, then the recipe *Getting files from Amazon S3* will not produce an output. Use the following instructions to set up uploading into S3.

Getting ready

Check the *Getting ready* section under the recipe *Getting files from Amazon S3*.

How to do it...

1. Get a path to the file you want to upload, and the bucket you want to upload it to.
2. Run the following command:

```
$s3->putObject(S3::inputFile($file), $bucketName,
    baseName($file), S3::ACL_PUBLIC_READ);
```

How it works...

The putObject function encapsulates all the hard negotiations with S3. The function calculates the file size, MD5 checksum of the content, content type, and other information, and sends it along with the file to S3.

The file will now be accessible through the browser at http://s3.amazonaws.com/ BucketName/filename, and anyone can download it.

There's more...

You can utilize the other options during object creation.

Sending additional information in file headers

Additional headers can be sent with the file. If you want to send any information along with the file, pass a fifth parameter to the function, which would be an array of values:

```
$s3->putObject(S3::inputFile($file), $bucketName,
    baseName($file), S3::ACL_PUBLIC_READ,
    array('latitude' => '39.92', 'longitude' => '-81.40');
```

Assigning object permissions

We created a publicly readable file. Our other options are:

Constant name	Description
S3::ACL_PRIVATE	Only the owner has full control of the file.
S3::ACL_PUBLIC_READ	Owner has full control; general public has read permissions (including accessing the file through a browser).
S3::ACL_PUBLIC_READ_WRITE	Owner has full control; general public has both read and write permissions, letting them overwrite the file.
S3::ACL_ AUTHENTICATED_READ	Owner has full control; users who have authenticated their request can read the file.

Deleting an object

Eventually, you may want to delete the object you've uploaded. That can be done with the following function call:

```
$s3->deleteObject($bucketName, $objectName);
```

See also

- ▶ *Getting files from Amazon S3*
- ▶ *Creating a bucket in S3*
- ▶ *Uploading DAM files to S3*

Creating a bucket in S3

The best analogy for a bucket is a disk drive or volume. Normally, buckets are created manually, and code is configured to assign uploaded files to the buckets. You can still create a new bucket with code fairly easily.

Getting ready

Check the *Getting ready* section under the recipe *Getting files from Amazon S3*.

How to do it...

1. Come up with a unique bucket name. Use the PHP `uniqid` function:
   ```
   $bucketName = uniqid('MyBucket');
   ```

2. Add the following code:
   ```
   if ($s3->putBucket($bucketName, S3::ACL_PUBLIC_READ)) {
        // Bucket successfully created, proceed
   }
   ```

How it works...

Bucket names are shared among all the users of S3, so once a name is used, it's reserved exclusively by the owner. Furthermore, bucket names become part of a URL. For these reasons, the name must be unique. If the URL doesn't matter much, then a random string works best.

The `putBucket` function effectively encapsulates the details, accepting only bucket name and permission level. Amazon creates the specified bucket, and makes it accessible to the general public. Any files in the bucket can be downloaded through a URL of the form: `http://s3.amazonaws.com/BucketName/filename`.

The bucket name should be unique, so try to append a random string to whatever name you choose.If the bucket cannot be created for one reason or another, an error will be thrown by the S3 class. If you don't want such an error to interrupt the flow of your script, be sure to wrap all S3 operations in a `try/catch` block such as this:

```
try {
...
    if ($s3->putBucket($bucketName, S3::ACL_PUBLIC_READ)) {
        // Bucket successfully created, proceed
    }
} catch (Exception $e) {
    // Do something with the error
}
```

There's more...

In this section, we will see how to create buckets in different locations, how to set permissions for a bucket, and how to delete a bucket.

Creating buckets in different locations

Amazon can create buckets in two locations—US and EU. US bucket is the default one, but if you want to create a bucket in Europe, you need to call the function with the following parameters:

```
$s3->putBucket($bucketName, S3::ACL_PUBLIC_READ, 'EU');
```

Setting permissions for a bucket

We created a publicly readable bucket. There are other options though, and they are the same as object permissions:

Constant name	Description
S3::ACL_PRIVATE	Only the owner has full control of the file.
S3::ACL_PUBLIC_READ	Owner has full control; general public has read permissions (including accessing the bucket through a browser).
S3::ACL_PUBLIC_READ_WRITE	Owner has full control; general public has both read and write permissions, letting them overwrite the file.
S3::ACL_ AUTHENTICATED_READ	Owner has full control; users who have authenticated their request can read the file.

Deleting a bucket

When you're done with a bucket, you can delete it using the following function:

```
$s3->deleteBucket($bucketName);
```

 You can only delete empty buckets—ones that do not contain any objects. Remove all objects first before deleting a bucket.

See also

- ▸ *Getting files from Amazon S3*
- ▸ *Uploading files to S3*
- ▸ *Uploading DAM files to S3*

Uploading DAM files to S3

Now that we know how to operate with buckets and objects in S3, let's adjust `dam_user_upload`, which is covered in Chapter 2, in the recipe *Creating frontend upload form*, to upload the files to S3.

Getting ready

We will describe the changes that need to be made to the `dam_user_upload` extension—it's up to you if you want to create a brand new extension, or modify the existing one. We'll assume the new extension is called `s3_upload` in the steps outlined below.

How to do it...

1. Create a directory `lib`, and copy the `S3.php` library into it.

2. Include the S3 library in `pi1/class.tx_s3upload_pi1.php`:

   ```
   require_once(t3lib_extMgm::extPath('s3_upload').'lib/S3.php');
   ```

3. Most of our functionality is modular, so we just need to replace the function `uploadFile` with:

   ```
   function uploadFile($title, $author, $description) {
       if (!$this->conf['accessCode']) {
           return 'Error: S3 access code was not defined in
             TypoScript';
       }
       if (!$this->conf['secretCode']) {
   ```

```
            return 'Error: S3 secret code was not defined in
              TypoScript';
         }
         if (!$this->conf['bucket']) {
            return 'Error: Upload bucket not defined in TypoScript';
         }

         // Instantiate the object
         $s3 = new S3($this->conf['accessCode'], $this-
           >conf['secretCode']);

         // Find a unique name
         $i = 0;
         do {
            $i++;
            $objectName = t3lib_div::shortMD5($i . $GLOBALS['TSFE']-
              >fe_user->user["uid"] . $_FILES['tx_damuserupload_
              pi1_file']['name']) . '_' . $_FILES['tx_damuserupload_
              pi1_file']['name'];
         }
         while($s3->getObjectInfo($this->conf['bucket'],
          $objectName));

         // Set object metadata into headers:
         $headers = array(
            'title' => $title,
            'author' => $author,
            'description' => $description
         );

         // Upload the file
         if($s3->putObject(S3::inputFile($_FILES['tx_damuserupload_
           pi1_file']['tmp_name']),
            $this->conf['bucket'], $objectName, S3::ACL_PUBLIC_READ,
              $headers)) {
            $content .= $this->pi_getLL('successful_upload');
         } else {
            $content .= $this->pi_getLL('failed_upload');
         }

         $content .= '<a href="' . $this->pi_
          getPageLink($GLOBALS['TSFE']->id) . '">' .
          $this->pi_getLL('back_to_form') . '</a>';
         return $content;

      }
```

4. Set the following TypoScript options in the `setup` field of the template, replacing the values with your access information:

    ```
    plugin.tx_s3upload_pi1.accessCode = your-code
    plugin.tx_s3upload_pi1.secretCode = your-code
    plugin.tx_s3upload_pi1.bucket = your-bucket
    ```

5. The rest of the steps for including the plugin on the page are the same as in the Chapter 2 recipe, *Creating frontend upload form.*

How it works...

Our procedure is very similar to `dam_user_upload`, but this time we upload the file directly to S3. First, we check that we have all the needed values—S3 access and secret codes, as well as the bucket name where we will upload the files. These settings should be set in TypoScript, and if they are not, we print an error message.

Next, we find a unique object name, using the same procedure as in `dam_user_upload`, but this time using an S3 function instead of PHP's `file_exists()`. Once we obtain a unique object name, we proceed with the upload.

There's more...

There are a few opportunities for improvement in this extension. Let's look at one.

Setting unique flexform options for each plugin instance

Instead of including options in TypoScript, these settings can be unique for each instance of a plugin. To make it possible, a plugin needs to have a flexform.

Another common approach is to make the flexform settings optional, with a fallback to TypoScript settings. That way specific settings can be customized for each instance of a plugin, but those that are not set will default to values from TypoScript.

Refer to official TYPO3 documentation for a thorough description of flexforms.

See also

▶ *Getting files from Amazon S3*

▶ *Uploading files to S3*

▶ *Creating a bucket in S3*

▶ *Creating a frontend upload form*

Getting recent Flickr photos

The Flickr API is very powerful and gives access to just about everything a user can do manually. You can write scripts to automatically download latest pictures from a photostream, download photos or videos tagged with a certain keyword, or post comments on photos. In this recipe, we will make use of the `phpFlickr` library to perform some basic listing functions for photos in Flickr.

Getting ready

Before you start, you should sign up for a free Flickr account, or use an existing one. Once you have the account, you need to sign up for an API key. You can go to **Your Account**, and select the **Extending Flickr** tab. After filling in a short form, you should be given two keys—API key and secret key. We will use these in all Flickr operations.

We will not go through the steps required for integration into extensions, and will leave this exercise to the reader. The code we present can be used in both frontend plugins and backend modules.

As was previously mentioned, we will be using the `phpFlickr` library. Go to `http://phpflickr.com/` to download the latest version of the library and read the complete documentation.

How to do it...

1. Include `phpFlickr`, and instantiate the object (modify the path to the library, and replace `api-key` with your key):

   ```
   require_once("phpFlickr.php");
   $flickrService = new phpFlickr('api-key');
   ```

2. Get a list of photos for a specific user:

   ```
   $photos = $flickrService->people_getPublicPhotos('7542705@N08');
   ```

3. If the operation succeeds, `$photos` will contain an array of 100 (by default) photos from the user. You could loop over the array, and print a thumbnail with a link to the full image by:

   ```
   foreach ($photos['photos']['photo'] as $photo) {
       $imgURL = $flickrService->buildPhotoURL($photo, 'thumbnail');
       print '<a href="http://www.flickr.com/photos/' .
           $photo['owner'] . '/' . $photo['id'] . '">' .
           '<img src="' . $imgURL . '" /></a><br />';
   }
   ```

How it works...

The Flickr API is exposed as a set of REST services, which we can issue calls to. The tough work of signing the requests and parsing the results is encapsulated by `phpFlickr`, so we don't have to worry about it. Our job is to gather the parameters, issue the request, and process the response.

In the example above, we got a list of public photos from a user `7542705@N08`. You may not know the user ID of the person you want to get photos for, but Flickr API offers several methods for finding the ID:

```
$userID = $flickrService->people_findByEmail($email);
$userID = $flickrService->people_findByUsername($username);
```

If you have the user ID, but want to get more information about the user, you can do it with the following calls:

```
// Get more info about the user:
$flickrService->people_getInfo($userID);
// Find which public groups the user belongs to:
$flickrService->people_getPublicGroups($userID);
// Get user's public photos:
$flickrService->people_getPublicPhotos($userID);
```

We utilize the `people_getPublicPhotos` method to get the user's photostream. The returned array has the following structure:

```
Array
(
    [photos] => Array
        (
            [page] => 1
            [pages] => 8
            [perpage] => 100
            [total] => 770
            [photo] => Array
                (
                    [0] => Array
                        (
                            [id] => 3960430648
                            [owner] => 7542705@N08
                            [secret] => 9c4087aae3
                            [server] => 3423
                            [farm] => 4
                            [title] => One Cold Morning
                            [ispublic] => 1
```

```
                                            [isfriend] => 0
                                            [isfamily] => 0
                                    )
                              [...]
                        )
                  )
            )
```

We loop over the `$photos['photos']['photo']` array, and for each image, we build a URL for the thumbnail using the `buildPhotoURL` method, and a link to the image page on Flickr.

There's more...

There are lots of other things we can do, but we will only cover a few basic operations.

Error reporting and debugging

Occasionally, you might encounter an output you do not expect. It's possible that the Flickr API returned an error, but by default, it's not shown to the user. You need to call the following functions to get more information about the error:

```
$errorCode = $flickrService->getErrorCode();
$errorMessage = $flickrService->getErrorMsg();
```

Downloading a list of recent photos

You can get a list of the most recent photos uploaded to Flickr using the following call:

```
$recentPhotos = $flickrService->photos_getRecent();
```

See also

▶ *Uploading files to Flickr*

▶ *Uploading DAM files to Flickr*

Uploading files to Flickr

In this recipe, we will take a look at how to upload files to Flickr, as well as how to access other authenticated operations. Although many operations don't require authentication, any interactive functions do. Once you have successfully authenticated with Flickr, you can upload files, leave comments, and make other changes to the data stored in Flickr that you wouldn't be allowed to do without authentication.

Getting ready

If you followed the previous example, you should have everything ready to go. We'll assume you have the `$flickrService` object instantiated already.

How to do it...

1. Before calling any operations that require elevated permissions, the service needs to be authenticated. Add the following code to perform the authentication:

```
$frob = t3lib_div::_GET('frob');
if (empty($frob)) {
    $flickrService->auth('write', false);
} else {
    $flickrService->auth_getToken($frob);
}
```

2. Call the function to upload the file:

```
$flickrService->sync_upload($filePath);
```

3. Once the file is uploaded, it will appear in the user's photostream.

How it works...

Flickr applications can access any user's data if the user authorizes them. For security reasons, users are redirected to Yahoo! to log into their account, and confirm access for your application. Once your application is authorized by a user, a token is stored in Flickr, and can be retrieved at any other time.

`$flickrService->auth()` requests permissions for the application. If the application is not yet authorized by the user, he/she will be redirected to Flickr. After giving the requested permissions, Flickr will redirect the user to the URL defined in the API key settings.

The redirected URL will contain a parameter `frob`. If present, `$flickrService->auth_getToken($frob);` is executed to get the token and store it in session. Future calls within the session lifetime will not require further calls to Flickr. If the session is expired, the token will be requested from Flickr service, transparent to the end user.

At this point, the application is authenticated, and can access methods, such as `sync_upload`.

There's more...

Successful authentication allows you to access other operations that you would not be able to access using regular authentication.

Gaining permissions

There are different levels of permissions that the service can request. You should not request more permissions than your application will use.

API call	Permission level
`$flickrService->auth('read', false);`	Permissions to read users' files, sets, collections, groups, and more.
`$flickrService->auth('write', false);`	Permissions to write (upload, create new, and so on).
`$flickrService->auth('delete', false);`	Permissions to delete files, groups, associations, and so on.

Choosing between synchronous and asynchronous upload

There are two functions that perform a file upload:

```
$flickrService->sync_upload($filePath);
$flickrService->async_upload($filePath);
```

The first function continues execution only after the file has been accepted and processed by Flickr. The second function returns after the file has been submitted, but not necessarily processed.

Why would you use the asynchronous method? Flickr service may have a large queue of uploaded files waiting to be processed, and your application might timeout while it's waiting. If you don't need to access the uploaded file right after it was uploaded, you should use the asynchronous method.

See also

▶ *Getting recent Flickr photos*

▶ *Uploading DAM files to Flickr*

Uploading DAM files to Flickr

In this recipe, we will make use of our knowledge of the Flickr API and the `phpFlickr` interface to build a Flickr upload service into DAM. We will create a new action class, which will add our functionality into a DAM file list and context menus.

Getting ready

For simplicity, we will skip the process of creating the extension. You can download the extension `dam_flickr_upload` and view the source code. We will examine it in more detail in the *How it works...* section.

How to do it...

1. Sign up for Flickr, and request an API key if you haven't already done so.

2. After you receive your key, click **Edit key details**

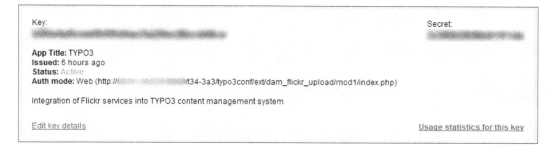

Key:

Secret:

App Title: TYPO3
Issued: 6 hours ago
Status: Active
Auth mode: Web (http://   /t34-3a3/typo3conf/ext/dam_flickr_upload/mod1/index.php)

Integration of Flickr services into TYPO3 content management system

Edit key details   Usage statistics for this key

3. Fill in the application title and description as you see fit. Under the call back URL, enter the web path to the `dam_flickr_upload/mod1/index.php` file. For example, if your domain is `http://domain.com/`, TYPO3 is installed in the root of the domain, and you installed `dam_flickr_upload` in the default local location under `typo3conf`, then enter `http://domain.com/typo3conf/ext/dam_flickr_upload/mod1/index.php`

 You're likely to experience trouble with the callback URL if you're doing it on a local installation with no public URI.

4. Install `dam_flickr_upload`. In the **Extension Manager**, under the extension settings, enter the Flickr API key and the secret key you have received.

5. Go to the **Media | File** module, and click on the control button next to a file.

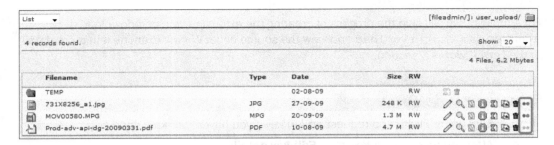

6. Alternatively, select **Send to Flickr** in the context menu, which appears if you click on the file icon, as seen in the following screenshot:

7. A new window will open, and redirect you to Flickr, asking you to authorize the application for accessing your account. Confirm the authorization by clicking the **OK, I'LL AUTHORIZE IT** button.

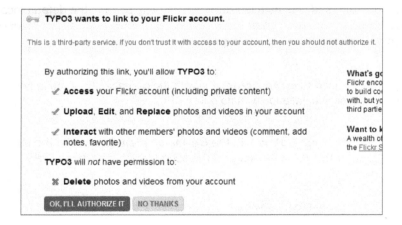

8. The file will be uploaded, and placed into your photostream on Flickr.

9. Subsequent uploads will no longer need explicit authorization. A window will come up, and disappear after the file has been successfully uploaded.

How it works...

Let's examine in detail how the extension works. First, examine the file tree. The root contains the now familiar `ext_tables.php` and `ext_conf_template.txt` files. The `Res` directory contains icons used in the DAM. The `Lib` directory contains the `phpFlickr` library. The `Mod1` directory contains the module for uploading.

ext_conf_template.txt

This file contains the global extension configuration variables. The two variables defined in this file are the Flickr API key and the Flickr secret key. Both of these are required to upload files.

ext_tables.php

As was mentioned previously, `ext_tables.php` is a configuration file that is loaded when the TYPO3 framework is initializing.

```
tx_dam::register_action ('tx_dam_action_flickrUpload', 'EXT:dam_
flickr_upload/class.tx_dam_flickr_upload_action.php:&tx_dam_flickr_
upload_action_flickrUpload');
```

This line registers a new `action` in DAM. **Actions** are provided by classes extending the `tx_dam_actionbase` class, and define operations that can be performed on files and directories. Examples of actions include view, cut, copy, rename, delete, and more. The second parameter of the function defines where the action class is located.

```
$GLOBALS['TYPO3_CONF_VARS']['EXTCONF']['dam_flickr_upload']
['allowedExtensions'] = array('avi', 'wmv', 'mov', 'mpg', 'mpeg',
'3gp', 'jpg', 'jpeg', 'tiff', 'gif', 'png');
```

We define an array of file types that can be uploaded to Flickr. This is not hardcoded in the extension, but stored in `ext_tables.php`, so that it can be overwritten by extensions wanting to limit or expand the functionality to other file types.

class.tx_dam_flickr_upload_action.php

This file defines the action class.

var $typesAvailable = array('control', 'context');

The `$typesAvailable` array defines the context in which the functionality can be used. In this case, we are allowing it to be used in `Control setting` (in the file list), and in the `context` menu. Other options include icon, button, globalcontrol, and multi. Refer to the DAM manual and source code to see how these can be used.

function isPossiblyValid($type, $itemInfo = NULL, $env = NULL)

This function returns `TRUE` if the rendering type is present in `typesAvailable`. Otherwise, it returns `FALSE`, and the action is made unavailable in the context.

function isValid($type, $itemInfo = NULL, $env = NULL)

This function is called for each individual file, and performs a check to see if the functionality should be enabled for the file. In our case, we check if the file extension is one of the allowed extensions:

```
$valid = in_array(strtolower($this->itemInfo['file_extension']),
$GLOBALS['TYPO3_CONF_VARS']['EXTCONF']['dam_flickr_upload']
['allowedExtensions']) ? TRUE : FALSE;
```

If the function returns TRUE, the action will be enabled for the specific file.

function getIcon($addAttribute = '')

The icon used by the action depends on if the action is enabled or disabled. If it is disabled, we show it visually by rendering a grayed out icon.

function getLabel()

This function returns a short label for the action.

function _getCommand()

This function returns a JavaScript action that is executed when the user clicks on the icon. In our case, it opens a new window, calling `mod1/index.php` with parameters corresponding to the file we chose to upload.

mod1/index.php

This module establishes a connection with Flickr through the `phpFlickr` library, authenticates the request, and uploads the file.

init()

`Init()` function initializes the class, and checks for the presence of the Flickr API key and the secret key. It also saves the parameters that have been passed in with the module call.

auth()

This function performs Flickr authentication, as described in the recipe above. As the request could be redirected to Flickr for further authentication, this function saves the parameters passed into the module in the backend user session. It is done using the functions of the `BE_USER` object: `setAndSaveSessionData` function to save, and `getSessionData` to retrieve the information.

main()

Assuming everything else went well, the main function simply calls the `sync_upload` function of the `phpFlickr` library to upload the file synchronously and report any errors. Another way the file can be uploaded is by using the `async_upload` function, which sends the request to Flickr, and proceeds without waiting for Flickr to index and store the file.

See also

- ▶ _Getting recent Flickr photos_
- ▶ _Uploading files to Flickr_

Reading list of movies from YouTube API

Working with the YouTube API is very similar to Flickr. We will use the `Zend_Gdata` library, which we can place in the `lib` directory. Let's now take a look at a simple task of pulling up the recent videos posted today.

> `Zend_Gdata` is part of the Zend Framework, but can be downloaded separately from `http://framework.zend.com/download/gdata`.

Getting ready

We will only cover the essential code. It's up to the reader to place the code wherever appropriate, and make sure all the needed libraries are included. For an example, look at _Showing video list using frontend plugin_ recipe further on in this chapter.

Before you start, make sure that the path to the directory holding the `Zend` library is in your PHP include path.

How to do it...

1. Load the required files:

```
require_once 'Zend/Loader.php';
Zend_Loader::loadClass('Zend_Gdata_YouTube');
Zend_Loader::loadClass('Zend_Gdata_App_Exception');
```

2. Set search parameters and send the request to YouTube:

```
// Initialize class
$youTubeService = new Zend_Gdata_YouTube();
$query = $youTubeService->newVideoQuery();
// Set search keyword/phrase
$query->setQuery('keyword');
// Set start index
$query->setStartIndex(0);
// Set maximum number of results
$query->setMaxResults(10);
```

```
// Set search types
$query->setFeedType('most viewed');
// Set search time
$query->setTime('all_time');
// Issue a query
$feed = $youTubeService->getVideoFeed($query);
```

3. Parse the resulting data:

```
foreach ($feed as $videoEntry) {
    echo 'Video: ' . $videoEntry->getVideoTitle() . "\n";
    echo 'Video ID: ' . $videoEntry->getVideoId() . "\n";
    echo 'Updated: ' . $videoEntry->getUpdated() . "\n";
    echo 'Description: ' . $videoEntry->getVideoDescription() .
        "\n";
    echo 'Category: ' . $videoEntry->getVideoCategory() . "\n";
    echo 'Tags: ' . implode(", ", $videoEntry->getVideoTags()) .
        "\n";
    echo 'Watch page: ' . $videoEntry->getVideoWatchPageUrl() .
        "\n";
    echo 'Flash Player Url: ' . $videoEntry->getFlashPlayerUrl() .
        "\n";
    echo 'Duration: ' . $videoEntry->getVideoDuration() . "\n";
    echo 'View count: ' . $videoEntry->getVideoViewCount() . "\n";
    echo 'Rating: ' . $videoEntry->getVideoRatingInfo() . "\n";
    echo 'Geo Location: ' . $videoEntry->getVideoGeoLocation() .
        "\n";
    echo 'Recorded on: ' . $videoEntry->getVideoRecorded() . "\n";

    foreach ($videoEntry->mediaGroup->content as $content) {
        if ($content->type === "video/3gpp") {
            echo 'Mobile RTSP link: ' . $content->url . "\n";
        }
    }

    echo "Thumbnails:\n";
    $videoThumbnails = $videoEntry->getVideoThumbnails();

    foreach($videoThumbnails as $videoThumbnail) {
        echo $videoThumbnail['time'] . ' - ' . $videoThumbnail['url'];
        echo ' height=' . $videoThumbnail['height'];
        echo ' width=' . $videoThumbnail['width'] . "\n";
    }
}
```

How it works...

The Zend_Gdata objects encapsulate much of the functionality, providing us convenient objects for working with the results. We provide our parameters, mainly the time span, sorting, limits on the results, and a keyword to search by, and the YouTube API returns a list of videos matching the criteria.

The $feed variable is an object of the Zend_Gdata_YouTube_VideoFeed class, which in turn is a collection of objects of the Zend_Gdata_YouTube_VideoEntry class. The latter has easy getter methods that we can use to get the information we need—such as video ID, title, description, category, thumbnail, and more.

There's more...

The API offers other options for narrowing down the selection of videos for a list. You can select the videos by placing restriction such as filters.

Filters

There are of course more filters than the ones we used. Here are some more functions you can use to set limits on results:

API call	Description
setAuthor($value)	Sets the list of the authors.
setCategory($value)	Sets the array of categories.
setFormat($value)	Sets the parameter to return videos of a specific format.
setLocation($value)	Sets the location parameter for the query.
setLocationRadius($value)	Sets the location-radius parameter for the query.
setMaxResults($value)	Sets the number of results to be returned.
setOrderBy($value)	Sets the value of the order by parameter.
setSafeSearch($value)	Sets the safeSearch parameter to either 'none', 'moderate' or 'strict'.
setStartIndex($value)	Sets the start index for the search results.
setTime($value)	Sets the time period over which this query should apply ('today', 'this_week', 'this_month', or 'all_time').
setUploader($value)	Sets the value of the uploader parameter.
setVideoQuery($value)	Sets the formatted video query (vq) URL param value.

See also

▶ *Authenticating requests to YouTube API*

▶ *Showing video list with frontend plugin*

Authenticating requests to YouTube API

Authentication with YouTube is very similar to authentication with Flickr covered in the *Uploading DAM files to Flickr* recipe, so we will skip on the details. It follows the same pattern of token pass back.

Getting ready

Make sure you have all the required classes already loaded (see Step 1 of *How to do it...* in the recipe *Reading list of movies from YouTube API*). In addition to the other two classes, load the `Authentication` library:

```
Zend_Loader::loadClass('Zend_Gdata_AuthSub');
```

How to do it...

1. First, you need to generate a URL to send the user to YouTube to provide authentication. The URL can be generated using the following method:

```
$scope = 'http://gdata.youtube.com';
$secure = false;
$session = true;
$returnURL = 'http://'. $_SERVER['HTTP_HOST']
    . $_SERVER['PHP_SELF'];
$url = Zend_Gdata_AuthSub::getAuthSubTokenUri($returnURL,
    $scope, $secure, $session);
```

2. Upon the user's return from YouTube, the request will contain a GET parameter with the token.

```
$token = t3lib_div::_GET('token');
if (isset($token)) {
    try {
        $sessionToken = Zend_Gdata_AuthSub::getAuthSubSessionToken
          ($token);
    } catch (Zend_Gdata_App_Exception $e) {
    }

    $_SESSION['sessionToken'] = $sessionToken;
}
```

How it works...

After the URL is generated, the user needs to click it, and provide his or her credentials to YouTube. YouTube will confirm that the user wants to give our application access to his or her data.

Assuming the user clicks yes, they will be redirected back to our application, where we will accept the token and store it in the user's session.

There's more...

Once you have successfully authenticated with YouTube, you can perform various actions that you couldn't do before. For example, you can post comments, manipulate playlists, tag videos, and most importantly, upload videos. The `Zend_Gdata` package provides enough information to get you started. As an exercise, try to recreate the `dam_flickr_upload` extension, but to upload a video to YouTube!

See also

- ▶ *Reading list of movies from YouTube API*
- ▶ *Showing video list with frontend plugin*
- ▶ *Uploading DAM files to Flickr*

Showing video list with frontend plugin

In this example, we will take everything we've learned in *Reading list of movies from YouTube API* and *Authenticating requests to YouTube API* recipes, and put it together to create a frontend plugin, which would display a list of YouTube videos.

Getting ready

We will be creating a new plugin, so make sure Kickstarter is installed. We will not go into much detail in plugin creation.

How to do it...

1. In **Extension Manager**, select **Create new Extension** submodule. If the option is missing, Kickstarter has not been installed. We will call the extension `youtube_connector`.

2. Under **General Info**, enter the basic extension information.

3. Click the plus icon (**+**) next to the **Frontend Plugins**, and call the plugin **Youtube**.

> The name of the plugin shows up in the plugin select box. If an installation contains a lot of plugins, it may get confusing for the editors as to which plugin they should use. Be creative in selecting a short name that uniquely identifies your plugin.

4. Check the box to create an uncached `USER_INT` plugin.

5. Click **View result**, and write to the location specified.

6. In the extension folder, create a new directory, and call it `lib`.

7. Copy the folder `Zend` from the library directory of the `Zend_Gdata` package into `lib`.

8. In `ext_localconf.php`, add:

```
// Add Zend library to include path:
$zendPath = t3lib_extMgm::extPath($_EXTKEY) . 'lib/';
set_include_path(get_include_path() . PATH_SEPARATOR . $zendPath);
```

9. Create a new folder `res`. In it, create a file `template.html`. Fill it with the following content:

```
<!-- ###TEMPLATE### start-->
<table width="100%" id="youtube_connector">
   <!-- ###VIDEO### -->
   <tr>
      <td><a href="###VIDEO_URL###"><img src="###VIDEO_
         THUMBNAIL###" /></a></td>
      <td><a href="###VIDEO_URL###">###VIDEO_TITLE###</a>
         <p class="videoDescription">###VIDEO_DESCRIPTION###</p>
          <p class="videoCategory">Category: ###VIDEO_
            CATEGORY###</p>
          <p class="videoTags">Tags: <!-- ###VIDEO_TAGS###
            --><b>###VIDEO_TAG###</b> <!-- ###VIDEO_TAGS###
            --></p>
      </td>
   </tr>
   <!-- ###VIDEO### -->
</table>
<!-- ###TEMPLATE### end-->
```

10. Replace the contents of `pi1/class.tx_youtubeconnector_pi1.php` with the content from the `youtube_connector` extension that can be downloaded from the book's site (`http://www.packtpub.com/files/code/8488_Code.zip`).

11. Add the plugin to a page, and preview it. Try passing in a few parameters to narrow down list results:

Apple's "Get a Mac" ad: "Tetter Tottering"

http://www.macdailynews.com To go from WIndows XP to WIndow customer satisfaction: Apple's Mac.

Category: Tech

Tags: **apple jobs mac ipod iphone app store itunes macbook imac**

CheapyD & CampingKev vs. Windows 7 Whopper

Celebrating the launch of Windows 7 in Japan, the Windows 7 Whop

Category: People

Tags: **burger king whopper cheapyd cheapassgamer cagcast jap:**

Seven Whopper Patties for Windows 7

How it works...

All the hard work is handled by the `Zend_Gdata` objects. But, we need to load it into our script. The framework expects the folder containing the `Zend_Gdata` objects to be in the include path in PHP. We could require the administrators to add the appropriate directory to `php.ini`, but this is error prone, and makes the job of administrators harder. Instead, we add the appropriate directory to the include path at runtime, while the TYPO3 framework is initializing. We added this to `ext_localconf.php`:

```
// Add Zend library to include path:
$zendPath = t3lib_extMgm::extPath($_EXTKEY) . 'lib/';
set_include_path(get_include_path() . PATH_SEPARATOR . $zendPath);
```

This does exactly what we just described. First, it resolves the path to the `lib` folder (under which the `Zend` directory resides), based on where the extension was installed. Then, it appends the include path with the location.

When we look at the plugin, one of the first lines loads the `Zend` class loader:

```
require_once 'Zend/Loader.php';
```

The script now knows where to find the file because we have told PHP where to look for files.

Now, let's look at what happens in the rest of the plugin.

main()

After we set some default parameters (these are generated by the Kickstarter), we load the classes we will need later:

```
Zend_Loader::loadClass('Zend_Gdata_YouTube');
Zend_Loader::loadClass('Zend_Gdata_AuthSub');
Zend_Loader::loadClass('Zend_Gdata_App_Exception');
```

Next, we initialize some variables based on the parameters passed to the plugin through GET variables or TypoScript:

```
$this->init($conf);
```

Finally, we get the content and return it to be printed on the screen:

```
$content = $this->renderContent();
return $this->pi_wrapInBaseClass($content);
```

init()

We start our initialization with gathering the GET parameters sent to the page that pertains to us.

```
$input = $this->piVars;
```

The parameters will be automatically available to us through the class variable. We then go through each parameter, typically checking the input value and using it if present, otherwise using the TypoScript value. If the TypoScript value is not set, we use a default. This allows for maximum flexibility, where the plugin output can be controlled by a combination of parameters passed through the URL and TypoScript. Let's walk through an example of setting the search type:

```
$this->searchType = isset($input['searchType']) ? $input['searchType']
    : $conf['searchType'];
if (!$this->searchType ||
    !in_array($this->searchType, $this->validSearchTypes)) {
    $this->searchType = 'most viewed'; // Provide a default
}
```

First, we check if `$input['searchType']` is set. This is the value sent through the GET parameters in a URL, like `http://example.com/index.php?id=21&tx_youtubeconnector_pi1[searchType]=top%20rated`. If it is not set, we use the TypoScript value, passed to the plugin, like `plugin.tx_youtubeconnector_pi1.searchType = top rated`

Neither of these needs to be present. Furthermore, parameters passed could be misspelled, or could even be an attempt to break our application. So, we run a final check to make sure we have a value and it's present in the expected values array:

```
var $validSearchTypes = array('top rated', 'most viewed',
    'recently featured', 'mobile');
```

If it's not, we give it a default value of `most viewed`.

renderContent()

In this function, we connect to YouTube using `Zend_Gdata` classes, and ask for a data feed using our defined parameters to customize it. We pass the resulting data feed to `renderFeed` function.

renderFeed()

The function starts by analyzing and extracting the template:

```
$template = $this->cObj->fileResource($this->templateFile);
$topTemplate = $this->cObj->getSubpart($template,
    '###TEMPLATE###');
$videoRow = $this->cObj->getSubpart($topTemplate,
    '###VIDEO###');
$tagRow = $this->cObj->getSubpart($videoRow,
    '###VIDEO_TAGS###');
```

`$this->templateFile` contains the location of the template file. It is set in our `init()` function, and can be defined in TypoScript. If the TypoScript value is missing, a default is used instead. The file is broken into appropriate subparts. Now, each variable contains a template, with markers and subparts that need to be replaced by data.

We go through each video in the video feed, extracting all the information we could possibly want. To make sure that we have a fresh start with each new video, we reset the `$markers` and `$subparts` arrays:

```
foreach ($feed as $entry) {
    $markers = array();
    $subparts = array();

    ...

}
```

Each `$entry` is an object, which has methods that let us easily pull the information we want, and place it into a marker array. We use the `htmlspecialchars` function on values to convert any HTML entities:

```
$markers['###VIDEO_TITLE###'] = htmlspecialchars($entry->
   getVideoTitle());
$markers['###VIDEO_UPDATED###'] = htmlspecialchars($entry->
   getUpdated());
$markers['###VIDEO_DESCRIPTION###'] = htmlspecialchars($entry->
   getVideoDescription());
$markers['###VIDEO_CATEGORY###'] = htmlspecialchars($entry->
   getVideoCategory());
$markers['###VIDEO_URL###'] = $entry->getVideoWatchPageUrl();
...
```

The list of tags is an array, so we treat it as such. We have a template for how each tag should be rendered, so we substitute the marker with the tag value, and append it to the list:

```
$videoTags = $entry->getVideoTags();
foreach ($videoTags as $videoTag) {
    $subparts['###VIDEO_TAGS###'] .=
        $this->cObj->substituteMarker($tagRow,
        '###VIDEO_TAG###', $videoTag);
}
```

We substitute the video template with the data we have acquired, and append it to a running list. Note how both markers and subparts (tags) are substituted here:

```
$videoList .= $this->cObj->substituteMarkerArrayCached($videoRow,
$markers, $subparts);
```

Finally, we substitute the list into the template, and return it. It will be placed at the location where the plugin was inserted on the page.

There's more...

This was just an introduction to the YouTube API, and to really have a functional application, you would utilize other features.

Displaying video

The plugin redirects the user to `www.youtube.com` to view the video. Of course, as a webmaster you want to keep the user on your site as long as possible. So, it makes sense to render the YouTube video in your template on your site. YouTube API provides enough data to show the video and related fields. We can even use the Media content element, which we covered in Chapter 5, to render the video.

Sending parameters to plugins

A recommended way of sending parameters in TYPO3 is to have them in an array, with the plugin class as the name. For example, to send a search term to our plugin on page 21, the URL would be `http://example.com/index.php?id=21&tx_youtubeconnector_pi1[searchTerm]=windows`.

A page in TYPO3 can have a number of different plugins, expecting a number of parameters. Passing parameters in this fashion prevents conflicts between plugins, and keeps them relatively isolated. Furthermore, the parameters will be automatically available to us through the class variable `piVars`.

See also

- ▸ *Reading list of movies from YouTube API*
- ▸ *Authenticating requests to YouTube API*

7
Creating Services

In this chapter, we will cover:

- ▸ Extracting metadata from OpenOffice documents
- ▸ Processing audio using a service
- ▸ Converting a video into FLV upon import
- ▸ Converting audio using services
- ▸ Building an audioConversion service

Extracting metadata from OpenOffice documents

Chapter 3 *Operating with Metadata in Media Files* recipes described how services work to extract metadata embedded in various files. There are times when no extractor exists for the file format that you need. In this case, you can write a service to extract that metadata from the files.

We will now cover how to extract metadata that is stored in popular OpenOffice documents. These files can be created in Writer, and have the extension .odt. This extension will also work for other files created by the OpenOffice suite, including .ods from Calc, and .odp from Impress.

 To learn more about OpenOffice, go to http://www.openoffice.org.

This is just one of the multitudes of services you can create. For example, you could create a service to extract the contents of a text file from various formats, or to handle user authentication, both frontend and backend.

Furthermore, you can utilize services in your own extensions, decoupling functionality from the core logic of the extension, and providing a freedom of implementation for the future.

Getting ready

To start, make sure you have Kickstarter and DAM extensions installed. Refer to the *Installing needed extensions* recipe in Chapter 1 for specific instructions. We will use the Kickstarter to create a framework for the extension, and then we will fill it up with code. You can follow the same procedures to create services for other tasks.

The metadata extractor will also rely on the ZIP support present in the PHP installation. Make sure you get the following output for **phpinfo()** to confirm that the needed support exists:

zip	
Zip	enabled
Extension Version	$Id: php_zip.c,v 1.1.2.38.2.29 2009/02/24 23:55:14 iliaa Exp $
Zip version	1.9.1
Libzip version	0.9.0

To test how our service is working, we need a test document with metadata. Use OpenOffice Writer to create a sample file. Click on **File** and choose **Properties**. Fill in some fields under the **Description** tab. Click **OK**, and save the document.

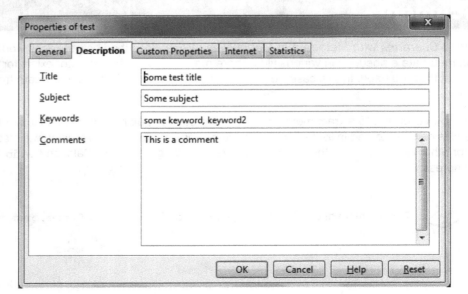

How to do it...

1. Go to the **Admin tools | Extension Manager** module, then the **Create new Extension** submodule.

2. Enter your extension key, and make sure to register the key so that no one else uses it. For this extension, you can enter `meta_openoffice`.

3. Click on the plus icon (**+**) next to **General info** to edit the basic required information about the extension.

4. Fill in the extension title, as the users will see it in the **Extension Manager**, and enter a brief description. For **Category**, select **Services**.

5. Under the list of dependencies, enter **dam**.

6. Click on the plus icon (**+**) next to **Services**. Fill the form as shown in the following screenshot:

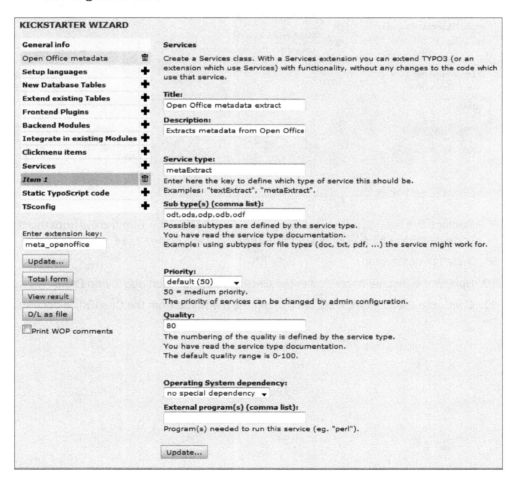

7. Click **View result** to see which files will be created. Write the files to the location you specify.

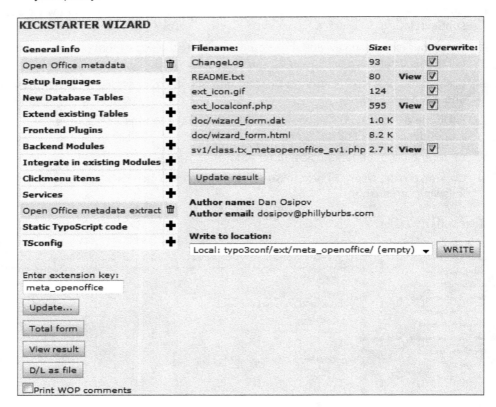

8. Replace the file `class.tx_metaopenoffice_sv1.php` with the file from the code pack (`http://www.packtpub.com/files/code/8488_Code.zip`).

9. Install the extension.

10. Upload the test file described in the *Getting ready* section above into DAM.

11. Check the DAM record. It should contain the metadata from the OpenOffice document:

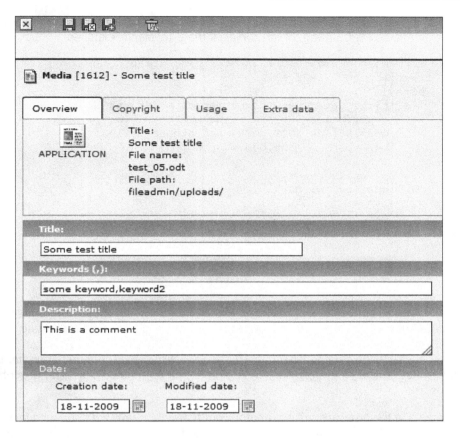

How it works...

In this recipe, we created a service to read metadata from OpenOffice documents, and store it in a DAM record, accessible to TYPO3. First, let's examine the way OpenOffice embeds metadata in its documents. There is public information about the OpenOffice format that provides enough information for us to know how to extract the data.

 An easy to follow presentation on the topic can be found at:
http://marketing.openoffice.org/ooocon2008/programme/
friday_1475.pdf.

The service we created is loaded into the TYPO3 framework in `ext_localconf.php`. Here is the code that makes TYPO3 aware of the service if the extension is installed:

```
t3lib_extMgm::addService($_EXTKEY,   'metaExtract',
    'tx_metaopenoffice_sv1',
      array(
            'title' => 'Open Office metadata extract',
            'description' => 'Extracts metadata from ' .
            'Open Office (ODT, ODS, and others) files',
            'subtype' => 'odt,ods,odp,odb,odf',
            'available' => TRUE,
            'priority' => 50,
            'quality' => 80,
            'os' => '',
            'exec' => '',
            'classFile' => t3lib_extMgm::extPath($_EXTKEY) .
            'sv1/class.tx_metaopenoffice_sv1.php',
            'className' => 'tx_metaopenoffice_sv1',
      )
    );
```

`t3lib_extMgm::addService` is described in the *Extracting metadata from images* recipe in Chapter 3, but we'll go through it again briefly. The first parameter sent to the function is the **extension key,** which is available in the variable `$_EXTKEY` in `ext_localconf.php`. The second parameter is the **service type,** in this case `metaExtract`. The third parameter is the **service key** that uniquely identifies our service. The fourth parameter is an array describing the service.

Most elements in the array are self explanatory, but there are a few that should be focused on. `subtype` lists file extensions that can be processed by this service. `priority` of the service determines the order in which it is called. We leave it at `50`, which is default. If an installation has several similar services, it can reconfigure the priority based on the quality of result that each service provides. `quality` value determines the value of the result. We make it higher than the default `50` because most of the metadata contained within the OpenOffice document can be scrubbed by our service. There are no special requirements for operating system (`os`) or external programs (`exec`), so these values are empty.

We now turn to the meat of our service— doing the extraction when a qualifying file is uploaded. A basic summary of the OpenOffice format tells us that the format is zipped, with the metadata embedded as XML. So, we need to unzip the file, and parse the XML inside of it. Let's see how we can do this.

init()

The `init()` function initializes the service class, and returns a Boolean indicating its availability. This is a final check before running the service, so, we need to verify that the PHP installation has ZIP support enabled. A good indicator of this is an availability of function `zip_open()`, which should be globally available if PHP is compiled with ZIP support:

```
function init()    {
   $available = parent::init();

   if (!function_exists('zip_open')) {
      // No ZIP support in this PHP installation
      $available = FALSE;
   }

   return $available;
}
```

process()

The `process` function actually processes the file (imagine that!), and extracts the metadata, returning an array of DAM fields, which will form the DAM record. First, we gather our parameters, and find the path to the input file:

```
// Get the file that we need to work on
if ($inputFile = $this->getInputFile()) {
...
```

Assuming we do have a valid path to the file we want to extract metadata from, we initialize an XML reader, and open the file as a compressed stream. This is why we use a URI-like path to the file: `zip://path/to/file.odt#meta.xml`.

```
$reader = new XMLReader();
// Read the Open Office file as a compressed strem
$reader->open('zip://' . $inputFile . '#meta.xml');
```

It will open the file, uncompressing it on the fly, and read the `meta.xml` file. Our job now is to go through it, element by element, compiling an array of metadata:

```
// Go through the XML elements
while ($reader->read()) {
   if ($reader->nodeType == XMLREADER::ELEMENT) {
       // We have an XML schema element
      $element = $reader->name;
   } else {
      if ($reader->nodeType == XMLREADER::END_ELEMENT
       && $reader->name == 'office:meta') {
         break;
      }
      // We don't have a value
      if (!trim($reader->value)) {
         continue;
      }

      // We have a value - we need to keep it in an array
      if ($element == 'meta:keyword') {
          $meta[$element][] = $reader->value;
```

```
        } else {
            $meta[$element] = $reader->value;
        }
    }
}
```

Array `$meta` now contains all the metadata from the file. We now need to map it to the DAM fields, and this is done by the next function. `process()` returns any errors that were encountered to indicate either a success or failure, letting the service engine decide what to do next.

parseMetaData()

This function uses a simple switch statement on each element of the array, assigning the matching value to appropriate DAM fields. At the end, the entire metadata array is saved in the DAM record, so that it is available under the **Extra data** tab, and is also available for any extensions that may utilize it.

```
foreach ($metaData as $key =>$value) {
    switch ($key) {
            case 'dc:title':
                $fields['title'] = $value;
                break;
...
            case 'meta:keyword':
                $fields['keywords'] = implode(',', $value);
                break;
            case 'meta:generator':
                $fields['file_creator'] = $value;
                break;
    }
}

$fields['meta']['openoffice'] = $metaData;
```

See also

 ► *Extracting metadata from audio*

 ► *Extracting metadata from images*

 ► *Processing audio using a service*

 ► *Installing needed extensions*

Processing audio using a service

We will now follow a few simple steps to create a service that will be called when an audio or video file is uploaded.

Getting ready

To start, make sure you have the Kickstarter and DAM extensions installed. We will use the Kickstarter to create a framework for the extension, and then we will fill it up with code.

How to do it...

1. Go to the **Admin tools | Extension Manager** module, then **Create new Extension**.

2. Enter your extension key, and be sure to register the key, so no one else uses it. For this extension, you can enter `cc_meta_audio`.

3. Click on the plus icon (**+**) next to the **General info** to edit the basic required information about the extension.

4. Fill in the extension title, as the users will see it in the **Extension Manager**, and enter a brief description. For **Category**, select **Services**.

5. Under the list of dependencies, enter **dam, getid3**.

6. Click the plus icon (**+**) next to services, to create a new service class. Fill it in as shown in the following screenshot (for an explanation of the fields, see the *How it Works...* section under the *Extracting metadata from images* recipe).

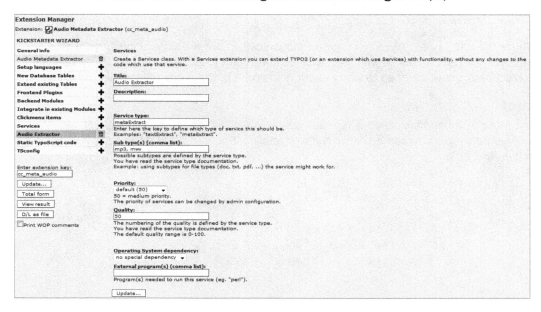

7. That's it! Click **View result** to see what the files will look like, and write the files to a location that you specify. You can now fill in the created files with your code and test how it executes. To finish this task, download the complete source code of `class.tx_ccmetaaudio_sv1.php` from (http://www.packtpub.com/files/code/8488_Code.zip) and replace the created file.

How it works...

In this recipe, we built a service that extracts metadata embedded in audio files, and stores it in a DAM record. We will now go through the file `sv1/class.tx_ccmetaaudio_sv1.php` and see how it works.

Include a getid3 class

This service will fill in a DAM record with metadata, so we need to ensure that DAM is installed. We will also use the getid3 library, available in TYPO3 as the `getid3` extension. Alternatively, we could have included the entire library in our extension, but creating a dependency allows us to keep our code simple, and easy to understand, and reduces duplication in case a user already needs the `getid3` extension for other purposes.

 For more information about the getid3 parser, see: `http://getid3.sourceforge.net/`.

This line at the top of the file includes the necessary `getid3` class:

```
require_once(t3lib_extMgm::extPath('getid3') .
    'classes/getid3.php');
```

Notice the `t3lib_extMgm::extPath` function call. There are several locations where the `getid3` extension could be installed, and we don't want to guess. The function figures out the correct path, so all we need to worry about is the path to the correct file within the extension.

init()

The `init()` function is called when the class is initialized, and runs a final check to make sure the service can be called. It must return a Boolean TRUE if the class should be called further.

```
function init()    {
    $available = parent::init();

    if ($available) {
        if (!t3lib_extMgm::isLoaded('getid3')) {
            $available = FALSE;
        }
    }

    return $available;
}
```

process()

The `process()` function is the main function of the class. The content of the file could potentially be passed to the function, which is why we have the lines:

```
// If we were passed some content,
// we need to write it to a file first
if ($content) {
    $this->setInput ($content, $type);
}
```

Most of the time, however, the file information will already be set, and can be retrieved by calling:

```
$inputFile = $this->getInputFile();
```

Whatever metadata we collect needs to be stored as an array in `$this->out['fields']`, where the keys of the array correspond to the TCA fields of the DAM record. We will fill in some of the fields further down.

If we do have the file information, we can instantiate the class `getID3`, and get the metadata from the file:

```
$getID3 = new getID3;

// Analyze file and store returned data
// in $metaData
$metaData = $getID3->analyze($inputFile);
```

`$metaData` now contains an array of information about the file. We need to transform it from the structure returned by getid3 to a structure understood by DAM and TYPO3. That's what the function `processMetaData($metadata)` does.

```
$this->out['fields'] = $this->processMetaData($metaData);
```

In order to signal success of operation, there are a few error capturing methods:

```
// See if there are any errors
if (is_array($metaData['error'])) {
    $this->errorPush(T3_ERR_SV_GENERAL,
        implode(', ', $metaData['error']));
}
```

This creates a general error, if it is set. Of course, if there were no file given, we want to issue a different error:

```
$this->errorPush(T3_ERR_SV_NO_INPUT, 'No or empty input.');
```

Finally, we need to return the last error to the object calling the service to let it know if we have experienced any issues:

```
return $this->getLastError();
```

If there were no error, `getLastError()` returns TRUE, indicating that the output of the service can, and should be used.

processMetaData()

As previously mentioned, `processMetaData()` transforms getid3 tags into DAM fields. `$data['tags_html']` contains the metadata we're most interested in.

```
foreach ($data['tags_html'] as $tagType) {
    foreach ($tagType as $tagKey => $tagValue) {
        switch ($tagKey) {
            case 'title':
                if (isset($tagType['artist'])) {
                    $fields['title'] = implode(' & ',
                        $tagType['artist']) . ' - ' . implode(' & ',
                        $tagValue);
                } else {
                    $fields['title'] = implode(' & ', $tagValue);
                }
                $extraID3Fields['title'] = implode(' & ',
                    $tagValue);
                break;
            case 'comment':
                $fields['description'] = implode(' & ',
                    $tagValue);
                $extraID3Fields['comment'] =
                    $fields['description'];
                break;
            default:
                $extraID3Fields[$tagKey] = implode(' & ',
                    $tagValue);
        }
    }
}
```

The reason we use the `implode()` function, is that the `$tagValue` could be an array, containing several values (for example, two or more artists). We need to account for this possibility, and merge them into a string. If it's a string, it will be returned unmodified.

Ideally, you would want to check the data type of the variable, and handle it accordingly. For example:

```
$fields['title'] = is_array($tagValue) ? implode(' &
', $tagValue) : $tagValue;
```

We left it out for the sake of simplicity.

After we have finished transforming, we keep the extra fields that don't directly match any of the DAM fields:

```
$fields['meta']['id3'] = $extraID3Fields;
$fields['meta']['audio'] = $extraAudioFields;
$fields['meta']['video'] = $extraVideoFields;
```

This way extensions can make use of this data, even if it is not directly usable by the DAM. The metadata is visible in the **Extra data** tab of a DAM record.

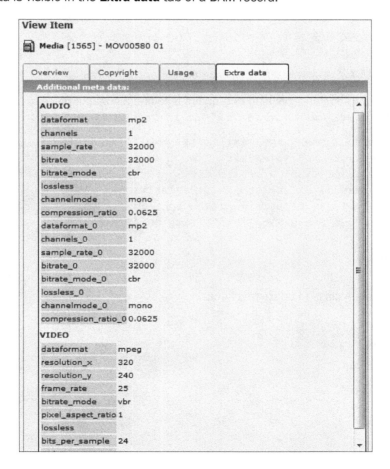

See also

▶ *Extracting metadata from OpenOffice documents*

▶ *Extracting metadata from audio*

▶ *Extracting metadata from images*

Converting a video to FLV upon import

One of the most popular formats for videos online is FLV. **FLV** stands for **Flash Video**, and integrates easily with the Adobe Flash Player and other SWF players, which has led to its success.

At this time, most video capture is done using other formats—predominantly AVI, but also MPG and MOV. In this tutorial, we will create an extension that will convert uploaded videos into FLV format.

Getting ready

We assume that DAM is installed for this extension.

The first step in approaching this kind of problem is to find a suitable place to hook into. The best place for this task is in class.tx_dam_tce_extfilefunc.php:

```
foreach($TYPO3_CONF_VARS['EXTCONF']['dam']['fileTriggerClasses']
    as $classKey => $classRef)        {
  if (is_object($obj = &t3lib_div::getUserObj($classRef)))        {
      if (method_exists($obj, 'filePostTrigger')) {
          $obj->filePostTrigger($action,
              $this->log['cmd'][$action][$id]);
      }
  }
}
```

We will now create a class to utilize this hook.

How to do it...

1.   Install FFmpeg.

We will be using FFmpeg to do the conversion, so make sure that you install it. If your system already has FFmpeg configured, you can skip this section. APT should install a stable version for us:

```
Shell> apt-get install ffmpeg
```

2. Create a new extension, with only **General info** data. Alternatively, you can place the functionality into an existing extension, but we will keep it modular.

3. Modify `ext_localconf.php`, adding the call to the hook:

```
require_once(t3lib_extMgm::extPath($_EXTKEY) .
'class.tx_flvConverter.php');
$GLOBALS['TYPO3_CONF_VARS']['EXTCONF']['dam']
['fileTriggerClasses'][] = 'tx_flvConverter';
```

4. Create the file `class.tx_flvConverter.php` and fill it with content from the code pack given in (`http://www.packtpub.com/files/code/8488_Code.zip`).

5. Upload a test file, and check that the FLV equivalent is created.

How it works...

Most of the conversion process is done by FFmpeg, and is completely transparent to us. For more information about FFmpeg, go to `http://ffmpeg.org/`.

ext_localconf.php

This file is included when the framework is initializing. Our call to the hook is declared at that time, so when a file is uploaded, the hook initializes our class and calls the `filePostTrigger` function.

class.tx_flvConverter.php

This is the main file of the extension, as far as conversion is concerned. Let's examine what each function does.

filePostTrigger

This function is executed by the hook mentioned above. The first thing it checks is if the action is **upload**—meaning the file is being uploaded—and file information is set. Empty upload file will still trigger the function execution, but `$id` array will be empty. Other options for action are **delete, copy, move, rename, newfolder, newfile, editfile,** and **unzip**.

 An interesting exercise would be to implement actions for other actions—for example moving the FLV when the original is moved, and deleting it when the original is removed. We'll leave it to the reader.

The function then calls the `t3lib_basicFileFunctions::getTotalFileInfo` function, which returns an array with basic information about the file including timestamp, size, type, permissions, and more. If the file is of the allowed type, the function calls the `compileExec` function, executes the command it returns, and passes the output to `processOutput`.

compileExec

`compileExec` creates the command that will be issued to the host system to convert the file. It takes a few options into account, and those can be configured in the Extension Manager.

The options are controlled by the `ext_conf_template.txt` file. This file has a specific syntax, which TYPO3 understands and creates the needed fields in the Extension Manager, storing the settings in `localconf.php`.

```
# cat=basic/enable; type=string; label=Audio Frequency
audioFrequency = 22050
```

The settings are then available in `$GLOBALS['TYPO3_CONF_VARS']['EXT']` `['extConf']['flv_converter']` as a serialized string, which we unserialize and store in `$this->config`.

Although we don't expect these options to contain quotes, or other strange characters, we pass them through the PHP `escapeshellarg()` function to make sure the command we create is shell safe.

processOutput

`processOutput` makes use of two functions to log the results. As the hook doesn't let us return any output to the user, we're forced to log it.

`t3lib_div::sysLog` is a system log used by TYPO3, which can be configured by the user to go into an external file, sent through e-mail, or written to an operating system, or PHP log.

`t3lib_div::devLog` is a log that can be controlled by extensions. We log the entire output of the command line to it. See *Debugging the extension* in *There's more...* for more information on how to acess the log.

There's more...

In this section, we will see how to debug the extension, clear cache, and look more closely at file conversions.

Debugging the extension

How do you debug if the file was not converted as planned? Install a `devlog` extension, and check the log after uploading a file. The log will contain the output of the command, and you can see where the problem is.

You can also use an IDE with the PHP debugger to make sure your code is executing properly. Refer to the Chapter 2 recipe *Debugging code*.

More on file conversions

FFmpeg offers a wide variety of options, to perform almost any format conversion you might need. For example, use the following command to convert MPG video into AVI:

```
ffmpeg -i inputVideo.mpg outputVideo.avi
```

Of course, this is not all you can do with FFmpeg. You can also use it to resize the video, create different bitrate versions of videos for your users, generate a thumbnail, or sequence of thumbnails from a video, and more.

Clearing cache

To speed up execution, TYPO3 combines the `ext_localconf.php` and `ext_tables.php` files into a single file. This increases performance because TYPO3 doesn't have to browse through the extension folders, including each file one at a time.

However, this means that any changes made to these files will not take effect until the temporary files are removed. You can easily do this using the **Clear configuration cache** option under the cache menu:

You can also turn off file caching in the Install Tool. The setting is `$TYPO3_CONF_VARS['EXT']['extCache']`, and you can set it to `0` to prevent these configuration files from being cached.

See also

▶ *Converting audio using services*
▶ *Debugging code*

Converting audio using services

Now, we will combine our experience from the *Extracting metadata from OpenOffice documents* recipe earlier in this chapter, as well as what we learned in the last chapter to create a service that would convert audio files upon import.

We will create an extensible system for conversions, providing only a few converters at first, but allowing many more to be provided by extensions, which will use—you guessed it—services!

For the user interface part, we will use Ext JS, which is available for use in TYPO3 backend since TYPO3 4.3. If you haven't heard about Ext JS, it is a JavaScript library, designed to make powerful **User Interface** (**UI**) layouts easy to create.

 For more information about Ext JS, go to `http://www.extjs.com/`. To learn how to use it effectively, I recommend a book *Learning Ext JS,* Shea Frederick, Colin Ramsay, and Steve 'Cutter' Blades, Packt Publishing.

Getting ready

We will be creating a new extension, so make sure Kickstarter is installed. This recipe will skip the details of how an extension is created, focusing instead on the important aspects. Refer to previous recipes (*Extracting metadata from OpenOffice documents, Processing audio using a service*) to get the detailed steps for extension creation.

The service we will create will use Mplayer, which is available in most package repositories and can be easily installed under Debian:

```
Shell> apt-get install mplayer
```

If you don't have access to Mplayer, you can use this opportunity to create a service that can use other methods for conversion.

How to do it...

1. Download the extension `audio_conversion` from the code pack.
2. Install the extension.
3. In the **Media | File** module, click on an audio file icon, and choose **Convert**.

4. Choose a conversion type, and click **Convert.**

How it works...

There is a lot that happens here, so let's go through it step by step. Instead of taking the usual approach used in this book, we will look at the plugin creation process from the very start, mimicking the path that you will have to take in analyzing problems and coming up with solutions.

Our task is to create a simple way for users to convert audio files to different formats within TYPO3. The system needs to be flexible enough, so that new conversions can be easily added at any point in the future. Conversions also need to work on different systems, regardless of the operating system, or installed software.

There are two major components to the task—the backend processing and the user interface. We need an optimal solution for both. Some tasks require you to prioritize one over the other, and implementation will vary based on which one is more important. That is not the case here, so we decide to use services for the backend processes, and Ext JS interface for the UI.

We will start with the UI, and work our way back to the backend. As we have chosen Ext JS as a framework for our interface, we already have a concept in mind. We've seen how easy it is to perform operations on files in DAM in the *Uploading DAM files to Flickr* recipe, when we added a control button allowing us to upload images and videos to Flickr. That button opened a new window, which sometimes required authentication. We want to use the same concept here, but want to avoid the unnecessary pop up.

We now come up with the user interaction component. In this case, it is very simple, but you should definitely draw a diagram for anything more complex. A user clicks on an audio file to bring up a context menu and selects a conversion option. An Ext JS dialog opens up, giving the user the choice of file types to which to convert. After choosing a type, the user clicks the **Convert** button, and waits for the file to be converted. The new file is saved in the same location as the old, but with a different extension, corresponding to the file type.

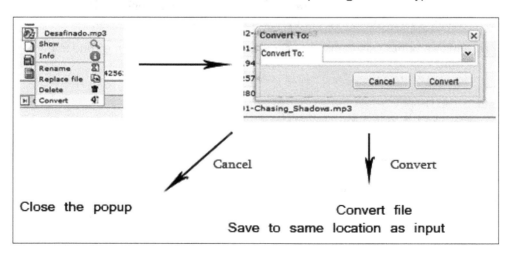

Please remember, that this is a simple demonstration exercise. In the real world, file conversion is never this easy, as each format has its own quirks and options, which may require a lot of knowledge and experience to be taken advantage of. In addition, each format brings its own specific advantages, which need to be leveraged by optimizing the parameters based on the intended final use of the file.

We start coding by mocking up an HTML page, which would serve as a testing ground for building the user interface:

```html
<html>
<head>
<title>Conversion UI</title>
<link rel="stylesheet" type="text/css" href="ext-3.0.0/resources/css/ext-all.css" />
<script src="ext-3.0.0/adapter/ext/ext-base.js"></script>
<script src="ext-3.0.0/ext-all-debug.js"></script>
</head>
<body>
</body>
</html>
```

The blank file just has all the components of Ext JS loaded, and it's ready for coding. We start by creating the familiar `Ext.onReady` wrapper in the `<head>`:

```javascript
<script language="JavaScript">
Ext.onReady(
function() {}
);
</script>
```

If it looks unfamiliar—don't worry! Follow along, and if something is unclear, refer to Ext JS documentation. It's a lot more intuitive than some other JavaScript libraries.

The first thing we want to display to the user is a window. So, we add some code to the `onReady` function:

```javascript
Ext.onReady(
function() {
    var conv = new Ext.Window({
        title: 'Convert To:',
        id: 'convwin',
        width: 300,
        height: 100,
        renderTo: document.body,
        frame: true,
    }).show();
}
);
```

If you save and preview the HTML page, you will see an empty, draggable window inside the browser:

That's exactly what we were trying to do! Now, let's add some content to it. Let's add a form with two buttons:

```
var conv = new Ext.Window({
    title: 'Convert To:',
    id: 'convwin',
    width: 300,
    height: 100,
    renderTo: document.body,
    frame: true,

items: [
        new Ext.FormPanel({
            labelWidth: 75,
            url:'form.php',
            frame: false,
            width: 285,
            defaults: {width: 200},
            buttons: [{
              text: 'Cancel',
            },{
                text: 'Convert',
            }]
        })
    ]
}).show();
```

Preview the file, and there will now be two buttons in our window:

Great! However, our buttons don't do anything yet. Let's add a select box:

```
new Ext.FormPanel({
    labelWidth: 75,
    url:'form.php',
    frame: false,
    width: 285,
    defaults: {width: 200},
    buttons: [{
       text: 'Cancel',
    },{
       text: 'Convert',
    }]

items: [
            new Ext.form.ComboBox({
                fieldLabel: 'Convert To',
                name: 'type',
                editable: false,
                displayField: 'name',
                mode: 'local',
                forceSelection: true,
                triggerAction: 'all',
                allowBlank: false,
            }),
    ]
})
```

Of course, an empty select box will not do us much good, so let's add a local store with a few options. These can be selected, and will serve as the choices for our conversion process. Eventually, we would want this list to be automatically populated.

```
new Ext.form.ComboBox({
fieldLabel: 'Convert To',
    name: 'type',
    editable: false,
    displayField: 'name',
    mode: 'local',
    forceSelection: true,
    triggerAction: 'all',
    allowBlank: false,

store: new Ext.data.SimpleStore({
        fields: ['key', 'name'],
```

```
    data: [
            ['wav', 'WAV'],
            ['mp3', 'MP3']
        ]
    }),
}),
```

Once you add this in, the select box will be populated by items from our array.

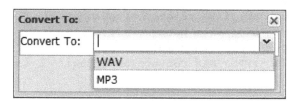

At this point, it's a good idea to share this file with your designer, your team, your superior, or your client, to get their take on the UI. Any input that will be provided at this early stage will help to avoid costly changes at the end of the development process.

We just quickly went through the process that may take you a lot of time at first, before you're familiar with all the options you can use in an interface. Even then, you may want to experiment with different layouts to see which one works best. Be patient, and you will achieve a great result.

Meanwhile, we've finalized the user interface, so it is time to integrate it into TYPO3. We've created the extension, and placed the resulting JS code (with a few changes, some of which we will highlight soon) into the res folder. So now, we need to add the button to the context menu. We add this line to ext_tables.php to register the action in DAM:

```
tx_dam::register_action ('tx_dam_action_audioConversion', 'EXT:audio_
conversion/class.tx_audio_conversion.php:&tx_audio_conversion');
```

And, we create the corresponding class:

```
class tx_audio_conversion extends tx_dam_actionbase {

    /**
     * Defines the types that the object can render
     * @var array
     */
    var $typesAvailable = array('icon', 'context');

    ...
```

```
/**
 * Returns a command array for the current type
 *
 * @return    array      Command array
 * @access private
 */
function _getCommand() {
    $file = tx_dam::file_relativeSitePath(
    $this->itemInfo['file_path_absolute'] .
    $this->itemInfo['file_name']);
    $onClick = "TYPO3.DAM.ConversionWindow('" . $file .
        "');";
    if ($this->type === 'context') {
        $commands['onclick'] = $onClick.' return hideCM();';
    } else {
        $commands['onclick'] = 'return '.$onClick;
    }

    return $commands;
}
}
```

You may notice that we call a JavaScript function onClick = TYPO3.DAM. ConversionWindow()—so that the window we designed only comes up when we click the **Convert** button in the context menu. We placed the function in its own namespace, to avoid conflicts:

```
Ext.namespace('TYPO3.DAM');
TYPO3.DAM.Base = function() {};
TYPO3.DAM.ConversionWindow = function(file) {
...
}
```

If we test the functionality now, we will get a JavaScript error. That's because the Ext JS library hasn't been loaded yet. TYPO3 provides an easy way to include Ext JS, along with the TYPO3 theme and adapters (which we will not use at this time):

```
$this->doc->getPageRenderer()->loadExtJs(TRUE, TRUE);
```

where $this->doc is an object of template class. Unfortunately, we don't have access to this object from anywhere within the tx_audio_conversion class, and there is no place to hook into in order to load the libraries.

TYPO3 provides one last method for modifying existing classes—**XCLASS**. This is not a preferred method, and should only be used as the last resort. XCLASSed class replaces the original class, and is called in all instances. We want to XCLASS the file modfunc_file_list/class.tx_dam_file_list.php from DAM. If you look on the bottom of the class, you will find an XCLASS inclusion:

```
if (defined('TYPO3_MODE') && $TYPO3_CONF_VARS[TYPO3_MODE]['XCLASS']
['ext/dam/modfunc_list_list/class.tx_dam_list_list.php'])
{
    include_once($TYPO3_CONF_VARS[TYPO3_MODE]
    ['XCLASS']['ext/dam/modfunc_list_list/
    class.tx_dam_list_list.php']);
}
```

This means that the last XCLASS declaration loaded is used. If several extensions attempt to XCLASS the same file, only one will succeed. This is the primary reason for avoiding XCLASS.

In this case, it looks like we have no other choice, so we create an XCLASS declaration in ext_localconf.php:

```
// XCLASS DAM file list module
$GLOBALS['TYPO3_CONF_VARS']['BE']['XCLASS']['ext/dam/modfunc_file_
list/class.tx_dam_file_list.php']
    = t3lib_extMgm::extPath($_EXTKEY) . 'class.ux_tx_dam_file_list.
php';
```

And, we create the XCLASSing class:

```
class ux_tx_dam_file_list extends tx_dam_file_list {
    function main() {
        global $BACK_PATH;

        $this->pObj->doc->getPageRenderer()->loadExtJs(TRUE,
        TRUE);
        $this->pObj->doc->JScodeLibArray['tx_audioconversion'] =
        '<script type="text/javascript" src="' .
            t3lib_div::resolveBackPath($BACK_PATH .
            t3lib_extMgm::extRelPath('audio_conversion')) .
            'res/tx_audioconversion.js"></script>';

        return parent::main();
    }
}
```

All this does is include the files we need, and return the content generated by the parent class method. Our class extends the original `tx_dam_file_list` class, so all functions available there are inherited by our object. XCLASSing can also be used to modify the output of certain functions and classes.

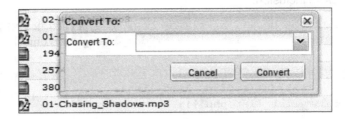

Now, we're able to get the plugin in the DAM file module, and it loads the window. Our UI is working as planned. Perfect! It is time to move on to the backend work.

If you look in the Ext JS declaration, we issue calls to `ajax.php`, and include a strange parameter `ajaxID`. This is a standard protocol for issuing AJAX calls in the backend of TYPO3. We have two calls that we need to handle—one to load the file types we can convert the audio file into, the other to perform the conversion.

For a detailed explanation of how AJAX calls work in the backend of TYPO3, refer to TYPO3 Core API: `http://typo3.org/documentation/document-library/core-documentation/doc_core_api/4.2.0/view/3/9/`.

We first register our two calls in `ext_localconf.php`:

```
$GLOBALS['TYPO3_CONF_VARS']['BE']['AJAX']['tx_audio_conversion::conve
rsionService']
    = t3lib_extMgm::extPath($_EXTKEY) . 'class.tx_audio_conversion_
service.php:tx_audio_conversion_service->convert';
$GLOBALS['TYPO3_CONF_VARS']['BE']['AJAX']['tx_audio_
conversion::conversionTypes']
    = t3lib_extMgm::extPath($_EXTKEY) . 'class.tx_audio_conversion_
service.php:tx_audio_conversion_service->listTypes';
```

And, we have to create the class to handle the AJAX calls:

```
class tx_audio_conversion_service {
    public function listTypes($params, &$ajaxObj) {
        ...
        $ajaxObj->setContentFormat('json');
        $ajaxObj->setContent($result);
    }
    ...
```

```
    public function convert($params, &$ajaxObj) {
    …
        $ajaxObj->setContentFormat('json');
        $ajaxObj->setContent($result);
    }
}
```

Let's implement `listTypes` function—it should get an array of file types the file can be converted to.

```
/**
 * Get the list of types that a file could be converted to
 *
 * @param    array      Parameter array from the AJAX object
 * @param    array      AJAX object
 * @return   void
 */
public function listTypes($params, &$ajaxObj) {
    try {
        $this->init(t3lib_div::_GET('tx_audioconversion_file'));
        $types = $this->getTypes();

        foreach ($types as $type) {
            $result['types'][] = array(
                'id' => $type,
                'ConversionType' => strtoupper($type)
            );
        }

    } catch (Exception $e) {
        $result = array(
            'success' => false,
            'errors' => array(
                'msg' => $e->getMessage()
            )
        );
    }
    $ajaxObj->setContentFormat('json');
    $ajaxObj->setContent($result);
}

/**
 * Return an array of file types that the file can be ocnverted to
 * Gather the types from all the services we have in the system
```

```
 *
 * @return    array       List of extensions
 */
private function getTypes() {
    $types = array();

    if (is_array($GLOBALS['T3_SERVICES']['audioConversion'])) {
        foreach ($GLOBALS['T3_SERVICES']['audioConversion']
         as $key => $info) {
            $requireFile =
                t3lib_div::getFileAbsFileName($info['classFile']);
            t3lib_div::requireOnce($requireFile);
            $obj = t3lib_div::makeInstance($info['className']);
            $types = array_merge($types,
            $obj->getTypes($this->fileInfo['fileext']));
        }
    }

    return $types;
}

/**
 * Initialize the class, gather all parameters,
 * throw exception if something is wrong
 *
 * @param    string      File which we want to convert
 * @return    void
 */
private function init($file) {
    $this->file = $file;
    $this->fileInfo = t3lib_basicFileFunctions::getTotalFileInfo($this->file);
    $this->fileInfo['abs_path'] = t3lib_div::getFileAbsFileName($this->file);
    if (!is_file($this->fileInfo['abs_path'])) {
        throw new Exception('File not found');
    }
    if (!t3lib_div::isAllowedAbsPath($this->fileInfo['abs_path'])) {
        throw new Exception('File location not allowed');
    }
}
```

As you can see, we first gather the information about the file we were passed, and make sure the file is in the web-readable space (otherwise, it would be too easy to break our application). Then, we call the function `getTypes()` to gather all services of type `audioConversion` (which, we created just for this purpose), and see which formats they can convert to, given the current file format.

All information we want to return (including errors, if such occur during the processing) is stored in an array. At the end of the execution, we tell the AJAX class that we want to return this information as a **JSON (JavaScript Object Notation)** string, which Ext JS can handle easily and efficiently.

We now turn to the most interesting part of this program—the conversion. At this point, you can get a list of file types that the file can be converted to—assuming you already created a service, so that when a type is selected, we need to do the conversion. We create the implementation in the `tx_audio_conversion_service` class:

```php
/**
 * Perform the conversion
 *
 * @param    array        Parameter array from the AJAX object
 * @param    array        AJAX object
 * @return   void
 */
public function convert($params, &$ajaxObj) {
    try {
        $this->init(t3lib_div::_GET('tx_audioconversion_file'));
        $conversionType = strtolower(t3lib_div::_GET('type'));

        // Security check
        if (!in_array($conversionType, $this->getTypes())) {
            throw new Exception('File Type not allowed');
        }

        // Do the conversion
        $success = $this->getServices($conversionType);

        if ($success) {
            $result = array(
                'success' => true,
                'msg' => 'Successfully converted'
            );
        } else {
            $result = array(
                'success' => false,
                'errors' => array(
```

```
                    'msg' => 'No suitable service was found to do the
conversion'
                )
            );
        }
    } catch (Exception $e) {
        $result = array(
            'success' => false,
            'errors' => array(
                'msg' => $e->getMessage()
            )
        );
    }
    $ajaxObj->setContentFormat('json');
    $ajaxObj->setContent($result);
}


/**
 * Go through the services to find the one willing to do the conversion
 *
 * @param   string      File extension which we want to convert to
 * @return  bool        Success or failure of conversion
 */
private function getServices($conversionType) {
    $excludeServices = array();
    while ($serviceObj =
    t3lib_div::makeInstanceService('audioConversion', '*',
    $excludeServices)) {
        $serviceObj->setInputFile($this->fileInfo['abs_path'],
        $this->fileInfo['realFileext']);

        if (!$serviceObj->checkConversion(
        $this->fileInfo['realFileext'], $conversionType)) {
            // Service not suitable for us, add to "ignore" list
            $excludeServices[] = $serviceObj->getServiceKey();
            continue;
        }

        if ($serviceObj->process('','',array())) {
            // Processed successfully!
            return TRUE;
        } else {
            $excludeServices[] = $serviceObj->getServiceKey();
        }
```

```
    }

    // No valid service for the conversion found
    return FALSE;
}
```

We go through the same security checks as before, and finally, get to the part where we find out what services we have available to us. `t3lib_div::makeInstanceService` returns only one service object that it considers to be best-suited for the task—based on the environment variables and the subtype we pass in through the second parameter. In this case, we don't use subtypes, so we pass a `'*'` string to match all the services of this type. Our services should have a `checkConversion` function, which will make the final call given specific file types, whether it's willing to do the conversion or not. If it is not, we add the service key to the list of services to ignore, and try to get the best service again. We perform this cycle, until either we find a service that will do the job, or we run out of services. The actual work of converting the file from one format to the other is left up to the individual services, and we cover it in the next recipe, *Building an audioConversion service*.

There's more...

We decided to go through each service until we find the best one. A more popular approach is to let TYPO3 do all the hard work of choosing the right service—which it does based on the availability of required functions and programs, as well as priority and quality levels set by the services. In that case, you can use the subtypes to limit the selection of services.

Using service subtypes

Services can define subtypes, which would simplify our code for calling a service. Specific subtypes vary based on the job at hand, and can reflect the file type, file contents, method of operation, and more. If you can make use of subtypes in your service definition, the code to perform service operations becomes much simpler. For example, here is the code from the `tx_dam_indexing` class, which uses a service to extract metadata from the file:

```
    // find a service for that file type
    if (!is_object($serviceObj = t3lib_div::makeInstanceService('metaExtra
    ct', $fileType))) {
        // find a global service for that media type
        $serviceObj = t3lib_div::makeInstanceService('metaExtract',
            $mediaType.':*');
    }
    if (is_object($serviceObj)) {
        $serviceObj->setInputFile($pathname, $fileType);
        $conf['meta'] = $meta;
        if ($serviceObj->process('', '', $conf) > 0 AND
            (is_array($svmeta = $serviceObj->getOutput()))) {
```

```
        $meta = t3lib_div::array_merge_recursive_overrule($meta,
            $svmeta);
    }
    $serviceObj->__destruct();
    unset($serviceObj);
}
```

As you can see, DAM allows TYPO3 core to find the best service for the job, and only asks it for the relevant output.

See also

▶ *Building an audioConversion service*

▶ *Extracting metadata from OpenOffice documents*

▶ *Uploading DAM files to Flickr*

▶ *Processing audio using a service*

Building an audioConversion service

In the previous recipe, *Converting audio using services*, we built a system that will convert audio files to a variety of formats using services. By itself, the system doesn't do anything, and relies on services to do the actual file conversion. We will now create an example service.

Getting ready

We will place the new service in the `audio_conversion` extension. If you've previously downloaded the extension, it should have the service we're about to create. Feel free to skip ahead to the *How it works...* section.

If you're creating your own service, make sure that you place it in a separate extension, and list `audio_conversion` under dependencies.

How to do it...

1. Define the service in `ext_localconf.php`:

    ```
    t3lib_extMgm::addService($_EXTKEY, 'audioConversion' /* sv type
    */, 'tx_audioconversion_sv1' /* sv key */,
        array(

            'title' => 'WAV',
            'description' => 'Converts to WAV',
    ```

```
                    'subtype' => '',

                    'available' => TRUE,
                    'priority' => 50,
                    'quality' => 50,

                    'os' => 'unix',
                    'exec' => 'mplayer',

                    'classFile' => t3lib_extMgm::extPath($_EXTKEY).'sv1/
                        class.tx_audioconversion_sv1.php',
                    'className' => 'tx_audioconversion_sv1',
                )
            );
```

2. Create the service in `class.tx_audioconversion_sv1.php`:

```php
class tx_audioconversion_sv1 extends t3lib_svbase {
    var $prefixId = 'tx_audioconversion_sv1';
    var $scriptRelPath =
    'sv1/class.tx_audioconversion_sv1.php';
    var $extKey = 'audio_conversion';
    var $validFromExtensions = array('mp3', 'mpg');

    /**
     * Return the types we have available for conversion
     *
     * @param   string      File type, from which to do
     * the conversion
     * @return  array       Array of file types, to
     * which conversion can be made
     */
    function getTypes($from) {
        if (in_array(strtolower($from),
        $this->validFromExtensions)) {
            return array('wav');
        }
    }

    /**
     * Do the final check for conversion to make sure
```

```
    * the service is capable of making it.
    *
    * @param    string       Make conversion from this file type
    * @param    string       Make conversion to this file type
    */
    function checkConversion($from, $to) {
        if ($to == 'wav' && in_array($from,
        $this->validFromExtensions)) {
            return TRUE;
         }

        return FALSE;
    }


    /**
    * Initialize class, and return if its available
    *
    * @return       bool   Availability
    */
    function init()    {
        $available = parent::init();

        return $available;
    }

    /**
    * Process the conversion
    *
    * @param    string       Content which should be processed.
    * @param    string       Content type
    * @param    array       Configuration array
    * @return   boolean       Success or failure of conversion
    */
    function process($content='', $type='', $conf=array())    {

        // If we were passed some content, we need to
        // write it to a file first (unlikely scenario)
        if ($content) {
          $this->setInput ($content, $type);
        }
```

```
        // Get the file that we need to work on
    if ($inputFile = $this->getInputFile()) {
        // Save the file to the same location,
        // same filename, but different extension.
        // WARNING: This will overwrite the file if
        // it exists, or fail if the file is protected.
        $outFile = substr($inputFile, 0, strlen($inputFile) -
            strlen($this->inputType)) . 'wav';
        // Build command
        $exec = 'mplayer -quiet -vo null -vc dummy' .
            ' -af volume=0,resample=44100:0:1' .
            ' -ao pcm:waveheader:file="' .
        escapeshellarg( $outFile) . '" "' .
        escapeshellarg($inputFile) . '"';
        // Execute command
        exec($exec . ' 2>&1', $output);
        // Write a log of what happened
        t3lib_div::devLog(implode("\n", $output),
        'audio_conversion', 1);
    }
     else {
        $this->errorPush(T3_ERR_SV_NO_INPUT,
        'No or empty input.');
    }

    return $this->getLastError();
    }
}
```

How it works...

Most of the information we learned about services before, still applies here. There are a few extra functions though, which are not present in the default framework file created by the Kickstarter.

getTypes()

This function returns an array of audio types that the file can be converted to. This function is called during the compilation of file types in tx_audio_conversion_service->listTypes.

checkConversion()

This function is called at the conversion stage, and is the final check to make sure file types are handled by the service. If this function returns TRUE, then the process function will be utilized to perform the conversion.

process()

The process function is relatively straightforward, and is very similar to the FLV conversion function (see *Converting video to FLV upon import* earlier in this chapter). Here, we build a command line call to mplayer program, and write the output to the devlog. As we have mplayer listed under the 'exec' section of the service information array we use during the definition in ext_localconf.php, TYPO3 will verify that mplayer is a program that can be executed. If it is not available, the service will be automatically disabled during runtime, and will not be used.

See also

▶ *Converting audio using services*

▶ *Extracting metadata from audio*

▶ *Converting video to FLV upon import*

8

Automating Processes

In this final chapter, we will cover some tasks that large systems may encounter, which should be automated. After all, that's what computers were designed for—the automation of tasks that previously required manual labour.

In this chapter, we will cover:

- ▶ Adding FTP access to the media repository
- ▶ Indexing downloaded files
- ▶ Setting up indexing rules
- ▶ Categorizing files by geolocation

Adding FTP access to the media repository

In the next few recipes, we will cover some FTP-related tasks, starting with the basic job of downloading files through FTP. This procedure can be used to synchronize files from a remote location with your website.

In this recipe, we will connect to `ftp.software.ibm.com`, which allowed anonymous access at the time of writing, and download the annual report.

Getting ready

Make sure PHP is configured with FTP support. If you go to the **Install Tool** module **phpinfo()**, you should see this output:

ftp	
FTP support	enabled

We will assume all directory paths exist—so if they don't, either change the values in the code, or create the necessary local folders (specifically ibm under fileadmin).

How to do it...

Create a plug-in, module, or a CLI script with the following code:

```php
$connection = ftp_connect('ftp.software.ibm.com');
$email = !empty($GLOBALS['BE_USER']['user']['email']) ?
    $GLOBALS['BE_USER']['user']['email'] : 'foo@example.org';
$login = ftp_login($connection, 'anonymous', $email);
$localDirectory = dirname($_SERVER['SCRIPT_FILENAME']) . '/' .
    $GLOBALS['BACK_PATH'] . '../' .
    $GLOBALS['TYPO3_CONF_VARS']['BE']['fileadminDir'] . 'ibm/';
$remoteDirectory = '/annualreport/2008/';
$list = ftp_nlist($connection, $remoteDirectory);
foreach ($list as $remoteFile) {
    // Difference between servers:
    // some prepend directory in the ftp_nlist,
    // others don't. Must check
    if (strpos($remoteFile, '/') === false) {
        $remoteFile = $remoteDirectory . '/' . $remoteFile;
    }
    $localFile = $localDirectory . basename($remoteFile);
    $success = ftp_get($connection, $localFile,
        $remoteFile, FTP_BINARY);
}
ftp_close($connection);
```

How it works...

We'll break the code down, line by line.

All connections to FTP servers must first be opened, and then closed at the end.

```
$connection = ftp_connect('ftp.software.ibm.com');
...
ftp_close($connection);
```

Once we've established the connection, we need to log in to the server:

```
$login = ftp_login($connection, 'anonymous', $email);
```

In this case, we're logging into a server that allows anonymous access, so standard authentication is username anonymous, and an e-mail address as the password. We use the e-mail of a backend user as the password, as that field is not mandatory, we fall back to a generic non-existent e-mail address.

If we were able to log in successfully, then we can download a list of files in a specific directory:

```
$list = ftp_nlist($connection, $remoteDirectory);
```

Finally, we're able to download the files:

```
$success = ftp_get($connection, $localFile,
    $remoteFile, FTP_BINARY);
```

This will save the remote file into the location specified by the $localFile. In this case, the folder contains PDF files, so we download them with a binary mode. The alternative is to use FTP_ASCII for text data.

There is one more line that requires some explanation—it's the $localDirectory variable. Here, we compile the absolute path to the folder where we will store the downloaded files, in a way that works across sites and platforms:

```
$localDirectory = dirname($_SERVER['SCRIPT_FILENAME']) . '/' .
    $GLOBALS['BACK_PATH'] . '../' .
    $GLOBALS['TYPO3_CONF_VARS']['BE']['fileadminDir'] . 'ibm/';
```

dirname($_SERVER['SCRIPT_FILENAME']) returns the absolute path to the directory, where the current script is running (for example: /var/www/typo3conf/ext/my_ext/mod1). We append the $GLOBALS['BACK_PATH'], which is the path from the root of the site to the typo3 directory. From there, we need to step one level back, and go into the fileadmin directory (which can be configured in the Install Tool). Now, we can append our folder where we want to save data, and our path is complete.

The path we end up with probably looks like this:

`/var/www/typo3conf/ext/my_ext/mod1/../../../../`
`typo3/../fileadmin/ibm`

Some systems have trouble interpreting the "../" steps back. TYPO3 offers an easy API function to take them out of the file path:

`$localDirectory = t3lib_div::resolveBackPath($localDi`
`rectory);`

To be completely strict, we should also use a backward slash if we're running on a Windows server. We can use the `TYPO3_OS` constant, which is set to `WIN` in a Windows environment, and adjust the directory separator appropriately. But based on experience, forward slash usually works well on Windows servers.

There's more....

We will now examine some things that we can do to expand upon this functionality.

Throwing exceptions

Any connection can fail for a variety of reasons—the server could be down, a network component along the way might be busy, or anything else. Therefore, it's recommended that we check that we have indeed established a connection:

```
$connection = ftp_connect('ftp.software.ibm.com');
if (!$connection) {
    throw new Exception('Connection to ftp.software.ibm.com failed');
}
```

Authentication can fail too, so we should provide some error checking after this step:

```
$login = ftp_login($connection, 'anonymous', $email);
if (!$login) {
    throw new Exception('Authentication to ftp.software.ibm.com'
        'failed');
}
```

File listing can fail too. The directory might be missing from the server, the connection could be dropped in the middle—nothing involving remote servers is reliable. So, before we use the file list in a `foreach` loop, we should check that it is an array:

```
$list = ftp_nlist($connection, $remoteDirectory);
if (is_array($list)) {
foreach ($list as $remoteFile) {

    ...

    }
```

```
} else {
    throw new Exception ('File listing failed');
}
```

What if we fail to download the desired file? This can happen for a variety of reasons—if the file is large the connection could timeout, the server might get overloaded or simply go down while someone is doing a reboot. We store the result of the operation in a variable called $success. Can you guess what we can do with it? The name says it all! In fact, try reading the next block of code aloud—it sounds very natural.

```
$success = ftp_get($connection, $localFile, $remoteFile,
    FTP_BINARY);

if (!$success) {
    throw new Exception('Failed to download ' . $remoteFile);
}
```

You would need to insert a try/catch block up the stack to catch the exception, and allow the program to exit gracefully, rather than with a PHP catchable fatal error.

```
try {
    // Do FTP work…
} catch (Exception $e) {
    // Log the exception, and proceed with the execution
    t3lib_div::sysLog($e->getMessage() /*message*/,
        'my_extension', 3 /*severity level*/);
}
```

This is the best way to handle errors, and TYPO3 4.3 provides an exception handler to make the error handling even more useful and user-friendly.

Downloading by date

If you run the task at regular intervals, you wouldn't want to download everything on the server, but only new or updated files. The easiest way to go about this is to delete the files once you download them. However, this is not always feasible, as you might be accessing a shared server, or may not have enough permissions to delete files.

In this case, you would need to find the date on which the file was uploaded to the server, and decide whether to skip it or download it. We will skip the decision logic, as it may differ based on the application—you may want to keep a record of the last run time, or schedule your task and download everything that was changed in between runs. We'll just take a look at how to determine the file date:

```
$rawFileList = ftp_rawlist($connection, '.', TRUE);
```

`ftp_rawlist` accepts three parameters:

- ▶ The FTP stream, created using `ftp_open`
- ▶ Path to the remote directory for which we want to get a list
- ▶ Boolean, which determines if the call should be recursive—include files in subdirectories

So, the call above is asking for a recursive list of files from the top directory. After it runs, `$rawFileList` will contain an array of lines of output that will need to be parsed into individual fields. Here is a function that can be used:

```
function parseFTPList($array) {
    foreach($array as $line) {
        $struc = array();
        $current = preg_split("/[\s]+/",$line,9);

        $struc['perms']  = $current[0];
        $struc['number'] = $current[1];
        $struc['owner']  = $current[2];
        $struc['group']  = $current[3];
        $struc['size']   = $current[4];
        $struc['month']  = $current[5];
        $struc['day']    = $current[6];
        $struc['time']   = $current[7];
        $struc['year']   = $current[8];
        $struc['name']   = $current[9];
        $struc['raw']    = $line;

        // fix for a bug where time replaces year...
        if (stripos($struc['year'], ':')) {
            // In this case assume current year
            $struc['year'] = date('Y');
        }

        $structure[$struc['name']] = $struc;
    }
    return $structure;
}
```

Output from different servers might vary slightly, and the function might provide incoherent results. Be sure to test it, using either a debugger (see the recipe *Debugging code*), or `print_r` statements on the output to verify that the output is indeed accurate.

Once the raw file list is parsed through the function, you will have a nice structured array with all the elements you need. From here, you can use the existing date elements, or even find the Unix timestamp of the file:

```
$structuredFileList = parseFTPList($rawFileList);
foreach ($structuredFileList as $file) {
    $dateString = $file['month'] . '-' . $file['day'] . '-' .
        $file['year'] . ' ' . $file['time'];
    $timestamp = strtotime($dateString);
    ...
}
```

Using scheduler for scheduled tasks

We wrote this script as a demonstration, but a common task is to periodically check the FTP server for new files. We can create a **CLI** (**Command Line Interface**) task that we can launch using a `scheduler` system extension at a specified interval.

Create a task file with the following content (name it appropriately for your extension, for example `tx_myext_ftpDownload`):

```
class tx_myext_ftpDownload extends tx_scheduler_Task {
    public function execute() {

        $connection = ftp_connect('ftp.software.ibm.com');
        if (!$connection) {
            throw new Exception('Connection to' .
                'ftp.software.ibm.com failed');
        }
        $email = !empty($GLOBALS['BE_USER']['user']['email']) ?
            $GLOBALS['BE_USER']['user']['email'] :
            'no@email.com';
        $login = ftp_login($connection, 'anonymous', $email);
        if (!$login) {
            throw new Exception('Authentication to' .
                'ftp.software.ibm.com failed');
        }
        $localDirectory = dirname($_SERVER['SCRIPT_FILENAME']) .
            '/' . $GLOBALS['BACK_PATH'] . '../' .
            $GLOBALS['TYPO3_CONF_VARS']['BE']['fileadminDir'] .
            'ibm/';
        $remoteDirectory = '/annualreport/2008/';
        $list = ftp_nlist($connection, $remoteDirectory);
        if (is_array($list)) {
            foreach ($list as $remoteFile) {
                // Difference between servers: some prepend
                // directory in the ftp_nlist, others don't.
                // Must check
                if (strpos($remoteFile, '/') === false) {
                    $remoteFile = $remoteDirectory . '/' .
```

```
                    $remoteFile;
            }
            $localFile = $localDirectory .
                basename($remoteFile);
            $success = ftp_get($connection, $localFile,
                $remoteFile, FTP_BINARY);
            if (!$success) {
                throw new Exception('Failed to download ' .
                    $remoteFile);
            }
        }
    } else {
        throw new Exception ('File listing failed');
    }

    ftp_close($connection);
    return TRUE;


    }
}
```

Add this to `ext_localconf.php` to make the scheduler aware of the presence of the task:

```
$GLOBALS['TYPO3_CONF_VARS']['SC_OPTIONS']['scheduler']['tasks']['tx_
myext_ftpDownload'] = array(
    'extension'       => $_EXTKEY,
    'title'           => 'LLL:EXT:' . $_EXTKEY .
        '/locallang.xml:ftpDownload.name',
    'description'     => 'LLL:EXT:' . $_EXTKEY .
        '/locallang.xml:ftpDownload.description',
    'additionalFields' => ''
);
```

You will now see the task listed in the scheduler **Information** submodule:

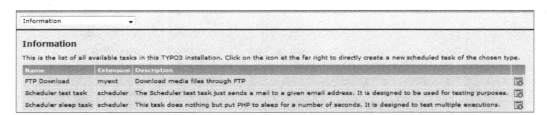

And you can create a new task, and schedule it to run at a specified interval:

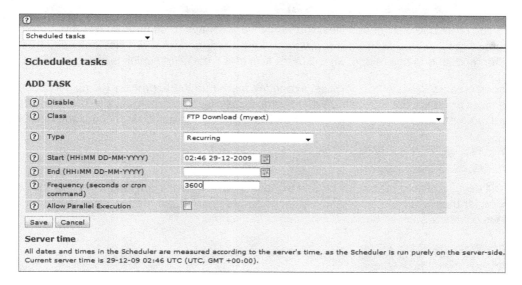

 For more information about the scheduler, refer to the scheduler extension manual.

Checking out other FTP functions

Just about anything you can do with an FTP client, you can do through PHP. Check out the full function listing here:

`http://us.php.net/manual/en/book.ftp.php`.

See also

- ▶ *Indexing downloaded files*
- ▶ *Debugging code*

Indexing downloaded files

Once you download the needed files, you would want to have them indexed by DAM. In the Chapter 2 recipe *Creating a frontend upload form* we already indexed files uploaded from the frontend, and in this recipe, we will index files in the backend (which is much easier!)

Indexing creates DAM records for files, extracting metadata in the process (using services). When files are uploaded through DAM, this process is triggered automatically, but when we download (or upload) files ourselves, we need to remember to ask DAM to index the new files.

Getting ready

We will design the code to work with and without DAM installed. Once again, we skip the steps needed for the rest of the code, and just focus on the heart of the matter. You can use this in various contexts, such as backend modules or CLI scripts.

How to do it...

Add the following code:

```
/**
 * Indexes a single file.
 *
 * @param       string          Path to the file on the server
 * @param       integer         Time of record creation
 * @param       integer         Page, where record will be stored
 * @return      integer         UID of the indexed file.
 */
function indexFile($path, $time = NULL, $pid = NULL) {
    // Set the page where the record will be stored
    $pid = isset($pid) ? $pid : tx_dam_db::getPid();
        // Set time when the record will be created
    if($time == null)
       $time = $GLOBALS['EXEC_TIME'];
        // Create indexing object
    $index = t3lib_div::makeInstance('tx_dam_indexing');
    $index->init();
    $index->initEnabledRules();
    $index->setRunType('auto');
    $meta = $index->indexFile($path, $time, $pid);
    return $meta['fields']['uid'];
}
```

```
Call the code with the desired parameters, for example:
if (t3lib_extMgm::isLoaded('dam')) {
    $damUID = indexFile($pathToFile);
}
```

How it works...

We are using DAM functions to perform the indexing, which is completely abstract to us. We initialize the class, followed by initialization of indexing rules. Rules allow you to customize some default behaviours of the indexing process. See the recipe *Setting up indexing rules* and refer to the DAM manual for a complete description.

Then, we initialize the `tx_dam_indexing` class, and set the run type to `auto`.

 Run type value is written to the log, and to the file record. It should be a four letter key that you can identify in case you need to find out how the file was indexed.

Finally, we call the `indexFile` function, and our file is indexed. We get the file metadata, as it was saved in the file record from that function, and store it in the `$meta` variable. You can then manipulate the variable, or proceed with your program.

Before calling the function, we check if DAM is installed—if it's not, we don't need to index the file (in fact, it wouldn't work):

```
if (t3lib_extMgm::isLoaded('dam')) {
    ...
}
```

This is a standard way of adding cross-extension functionality, without adding the extension to the list of dependencies.

There's more...

There are systems that allow FTP access to the `fileadmin` directory (see *Setting up FTP access* recipe in Chapter 2). The files that are uploaded through FTP will not be indexed, but you can index all new files on a schedule using the extension `dam_cron`.

Using dam_cron

If you have an automatic process outside of TYPO3 downloading files, or you allow FTP access to the `admin` folder, files will stay unindexed. New versions of DAM will auto index files when you go to a directory, but this requires human action. We can also set up `dam_cron` to index files on a schedule:

1. Install the latest version of `dam_cron`.

2. Enable the `cron` script in the extension settings:

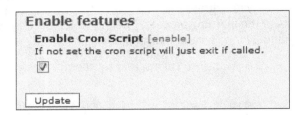

3. Configure an indexing rule in **Media | Tools | Cron Job**. Go through the four steps to set up an indexing configuration—specifically, the starting point, fields, initial values, and more. After the last step, you will be prompted to save the configuration.

 Remember the location of the file where you save it—you will need to use it in the task setup.

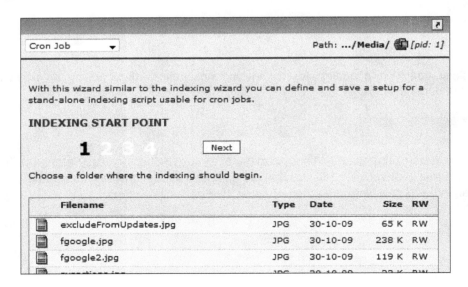

4. Create a new backend user with a username `_cli_txdamcronml`, and a random password. Make sure to give the user access to all DAM modules and tables, and add the `Media` SysFolder under DB mounts.

 If you have an installation with several cron jobs, or you foresee them in the future, I highly recommend creating a backend user group, exclusively for cron job users. This would greatly simplify rights management, and frequently save you headaches from trying to figure out permission errors in the logs.

5. Finally, set up a cron call to the CLI script, with the indexing rules parameter. For example:

```
/usr/bin/php /var/www/typo3conf/ext/dam_cron/cron/dam_indexer.
php --setup=/var/www/dam/uploads/tx_damcron/example.xml
```

 Refer to the `dam_cron` manual for more information on how it needs to be set up in different environments. It ships with the extension, but is also available here: `http://typo3.org/documentation/document-library/extension-manuals/dam_cron/1.0.2/view/`.

See also

▶ *Setting up indexing rules*

▶ *Setting up FTP access*

▶ *Categorizing files by geolocation*

▶ *Creating a frontend upload form*

Setting up indexing rules

We already mentioned briefly the indexing rules that can be set up in the *Indexing downloaded files* recipe; however, we will now go into more detail about how they can be set up, and what you can use them for.

Getting ready

Make sure both the extensions DAM and `dam_index` are installed.

How to do it...

1. Go to **Media | Tools | Indexing Setup.**
2. In the file tree, select the folder that you would like to be the starting point for indexing. Click **Next.**
3. In Step 2, check the option **Dry run.**
4. Skip Step 3 and 4.
5. In the last step, copy the XML from the textbox.

```
<phparray>
    <pid>1</pid>
    <pathlist type="array">
        <numIndex index="0">fileadmin/</numIndex>
    </pathlist>
    <recursive>0</recursive>
    <ruleConf type="array">
        <tx_damindex_rule_recursive type="array">
            <enabled>0</enabled>
        </tx_damindex_rule_recursive>
        <tx_damindex_rule_folderAsCat type="array">
            <enabled>0</enabled>
            <fuzzy>0</fuzzy>
            <createCategory>0</createCategory>
        </tx_damindex_rule_folderAsCat>
        <tx_damindex_rule_doReindexing type="array">
```

6. **Edit page properties** on the `Media` SysFolder, and in the **TSconfig** field, enter the following:

```
tx_dam.indexing.defaultSetup (
<phparray>
    . . .
</phparray>
)
```

Substituting the XML that you got in the last step.

How it works...

Files uploaded through the **Media | File** module are indexed one by one. **Media | Indexing** module provided by the `dam_index` extension, allows multiple files—even entire folders and subfolders to be indexed at once.

We have just walked through a series of steps to create a configuration that the indexing process will use. However, there are a lot more options that we can set.

There's more...

We will now cover the steps that we have skipped, and what we could do with their help.

Setting more options in Step 2

Step 2 gives a lot of options to customize the result of the indexing process:

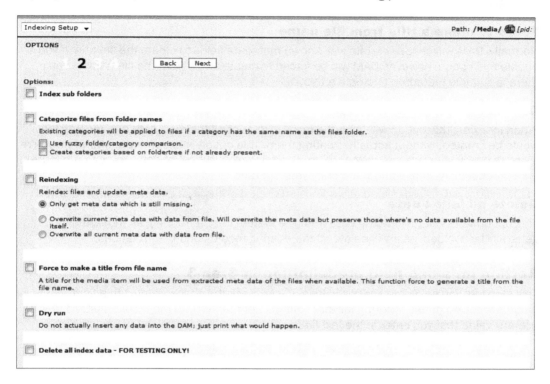

Index sub folders

Enable this setting if you want to index files recursively—in the current folder, and all subfolders. If disabled, only the files in the folder you selected in Step 1 will be indexed.

Categorize files from folder names

Enable this option to assign categories to DAM records, based on the file tree. If you already have a category tree that loosely matches the folder tree you're about to index, enable the fuzzy folder/category comparison. If you don't have a category tree, and would like to create one to match the folder tree, check the second option.

Reindexing

If the files have already been indexed, but you would like to index them again, check this option. If you believe the files have new metadata that is not present in the DAM record, select the first option to only get metadata that is missing. Select the second option to overwrite the metadata in the record with the data from the file, but preserve the data in the record that is no longer present in the file. Select the third option if you would like to completely replace the DAM record with metadata from the file.

Force to make a title from file name

Normally, DAM will choose certain well known metadata fields to create the file title. If you enable this option, however, DAM will be forced to create a title from the file name, even if there is suitable metadata to create a title.

Dry run

When indexing, this option will force the module to print all the metadata and records that would be created, without actually creating them. This option is extremely useful when you're trying to check your rules as they apply to a certain set or subset of data. You can run indexing on a production system without affecting your operations.

Delete all index data

This option will clear all indexing data from the system prior to running an index. It should generally be avoided, as it will delete all the existing records and their relations.

Setting indexing field predefinition in Step 3

This step lets you set some specific values. If you check the checkbox next to a field, whatever input is received during indexing for that field will not make it into the record. Instead, it will use any value that you enter in the text field.

Indexing Setup ▾

INDEXING FIELD PREDEFINITION

1 2 **3** 4   [Back]   [Next]

Preset meta descriptions for files.
The content may be replaced by meta content from the files themselves.

▼ Check the fields you want to set **fixed**.
The input will then not be replaced.

Title:
☐ [_____]

Keywords (,):
☐ [_____]

Description:
☐ [_____]

Caption:
☐ [_____]

Alt Text (www):
☐ [_____]

Source/Original location:
☐ [_____]

Source/Original location description:
☐ [_____]

Ident key (sku):
☐ [_____]

Creator:
☐ [_____]

Publisher:
☐ [_____]

Copyright:
☐ [_____]

Instruction/Usage:
☐ [_____]

Creation date:
☐ [____]

Modified date:
☐ [____]

Location description:
☐ [_____]

Location country:
☐ [▾]

Location city:
☐ [_____]

Content language:
☐ [▾]

Categories:
Selected: Items:

☐ [_____]
   ⊟ Categories
     ⊟ Photogallery
       ⊟ Photogallery
         Penguins
         Steelers
       ⊞ Sally Maxson

Indexing setup summary in Step 4

This last step gives an overview of everything you have selected, and gives you one last chance to change it before proceeding with creating the rule set:

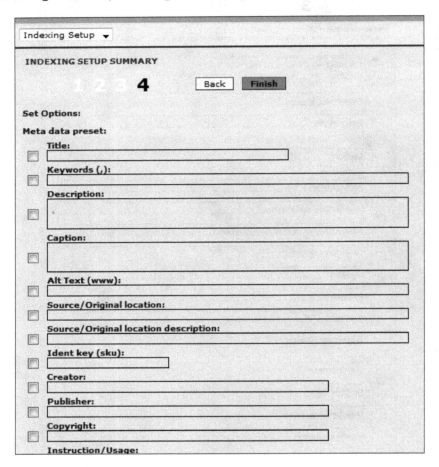

Setting more TSconfig options

There are a few more TSconfig options you could set.

tx_dam.indexing.skipFileTypes

This setting allows you to skip files of certain types from being indexed. Just enter a list of file extensions to prevent them from being indexed.

tx_dam.indexing.auto

If this is enabled (set to 1), files will be auto indexed. Auto indexing will happen when you browse to a folder containing unindexed files using the **Media | File** module.

tx_dam.indexing.autoMaxInteractive

This setting is only relevant if auto indexing is turned on. Indexing is an intensive task, using a lot of processing power and time. This setting places a limit on how many files can be indexed at a time. So, if a directory contains thousands of unindexed files, only a few will be indexed at a time.

tx_dam.indexing.replaceFile.reindexingMode

When replacing a file with another file, you can choose to either keep the DAM record from the previous file, or index the new file, and replace the information in the record with the data from the new file.

tx_dam.indexing.editFile.reindexingMode

This is same as the setting above, but applies when the file is edited within DAM.

tx_dam.indexing.useInternalMimeList

This uses internal MIME type to file type conversion list. In new versions of DAM, this list can be accessed and modified in **Media | Tools | Media types.**

tx_dam.indexing.useMimeContentType

This uses PHP function `mime_content_type` to determine whether a file is of MIME type.

tx_dam.indexing.useFileCommand

If MIME type couldn't be found using the previous two methods, this option lets DAM find file of MIME type using a call to the operating system (Linux only).

 Refer to the DAM extension manual for more options and their descriptions.

See also

- ▸ *Categorizing files by geolocation*
- ▸ *Indexing downloaded files*

Categorizing files by geolocation

DAM offers even more rules that can be used to modify the DAM record before it enters the database. Suppose your site deals with a lot of photographs, submitted by editors from all over the world. Images have good metadata describing the location of the shot, stored in IPTC tags. In this recipe, we will create a rule to add a category to these images based on the location where they were taken.

We will also use a different method for extending TYPO3—we will not create an extension, but rather make all the needed changes in the local instance. This makes sense in cases of specialized snippets of code that are not easily reusable, or are simply unique in their nature.

Getting ready

We will use the embedded metadata specifying the country and city to select an appropriate category. To fully test this code, you need to have a category tree with several countries, and their corresponding cities, and the files with embedded metadata that matches these locations.

How to do it...

1. In `localconf.php` (under `typo3conf` folder), add the following code:

```
$GLOBALS['TYPO3_CONF_VARS']['EXTCONF']['dam']
['indexRuleClasses']['dam_location_rule'] =
    'fileadmin/class.tx_damlocationrule.php:&user_damlocationrule';
```

2. Create a new file `fileadmin/class.tx_damlocationrule.php` with the following content:

```php
<?php
class user_damlocationrule {
    var $writeDevLog;
    var $setup = array(
        'enabled' => TRUE
    );

    public function preIndexing() {
        // Nothing to do
    }

    public function postIndexing(&$infoList) {
        // Nothing to do
    }

    public function processMeta(&$meta, &$path, &$indexObj) {
        $parentUIDres =
```

```
        $GLOBALS['TYPO3_DB']->exec_SELECTquery('uid',
            'tx_dam_cat', 'title=' .
        $GLOBALS['TYPO3_DB']->fullQuoteStr(
            $meta['fields']['loc_country'],
            'tx_dam_cat'));
        $parentUIDRec =
            $GLOBALS['TYPO3_DB']->sql_fetch_assoc($parentUIDres);
        $parentUID = intval($parentUIDRec['uid']);
        if ($parentUID) {
            $categoryRes= $GLOBALS['TYPO3_DB']->exec_
                SELECTquery('uid', 'tx_dam_cat',
                'title=' . $GLOBALS['TYPO3_DB']-
                >fullQuoteStr($meta['fields']['loc_city'],
                'tx_dam_cat') . ' AND pid=' . $parentUID);
            $categoryRec = $GLOBALS['TYPO3_DB']->sql_fetch_
                assoc($categoryRes);
            $meta['fields']['category'] .=
                intval($categoryRec['uid']) . ',';
        }

        return $meta;
    }

}
?>
```

How it works...

This class is loaded into a rule set that is used by DAM during indexing. The function `processMeta` is executed after the metadata has been extracted from the file, but before it has been written to the DAM record. In this function, we query the database for categories matching our specification.

There's more...

This simple classification can be extended to cover a variety of scenarios. Here are a few more tools for your arsenal:

Post processing

Another rule function is executed after the record has been inserted into the database. To make use of this hook, implement `postProcessMeta` function in your class. For example:

```
public function postProcessMeta(&$meta, &$path, &$indexObj) {
    ...
}
```

Creating new categories

As an alternative to creating the categories yourself, you can create them "on demand". When a file with a specific location comes in, and there is no category for it, such a category could be created with some default values and assigned to the DAM record. We leave the implementation of this as an exercise for the reader.

See also

► *Setting up indexing rules*

► *Indexing downloaded files*

Index

Thank you for buying
TYPO3 4.3 Multimedia Cookbook

Packt Open Source Project Royalties

When we sell a book written on an Open Source project, we pay a royalty directly to that project. Therefore by purchasing TYPO3 4.3 Multimedia Cookbook, Packt will have given some of the money received to the TYPO3 project.

In the long term, we see ourselves and you—customers and readers of our books—as part of the Open Source ecosystem, providing sustainable revenue for the projects we publish on. Our aim at Packt is to establish publishing royalties as an essential part of the service and support a business model that sustains Open Source.

If you're working with an Open Source project that you would like us to publish on, and subsequently pay royalties to, please get in touch with us.

Writing for Packt

We welcome all inquiries from people who are interested in authoring. Book proposals should be sent to author@packtpub.com. If your book idea is still at an early stage and you would like to discuss it first before writing a formal book proposal, contact us; one of our commissioning editors will get in touch with you.

We're not just looking for published authors; if you have strong technical skills but no writing experience, our experienced editors can help you develop a writing career, or simply get some additional reward for your expertise.

About Packt Publishing

Packt, pronounced 'packed', published its first book "Mastering phpMyAdmin for Effective MySQL Management" in April 2004 and subsequently continued to specialize in publishing highly focused books on specific technologies and solutions.

Our books and publications share the experiences of your fellow IT professionals in adapting and customizing today's systems, applications, and frameworks. Our solution-based books give you the knowledge and power to customize the software and technologies you're using to get the job done. Packt books are more specific and less general than the IT books you have seen in the past. Our unique business model allows us to bring you more focused information, giving you more of what you need to know, and less of what you don't.

Packt is a modern, yet unique publishing company, which focuses on producing quality, cutting-edge books for communities of developers, administrators, and newbies alike. For more information, please visit our website: www.PacktPub.com.

Building Websites with TYPO3

ISBN: 978-1-847191-11-3 Paperback: 208 pages

A practical step-by-step tutorial to creating your TYPO3 website

1. A practical step-by-step tutorial to creating your TYPO3 website

2. Install and configure TYPO3

3. Master all the important aspects of TYPO3, including the backend, the frontend, content management, and templates

4. Gain hands-on experience by developing an example site through the book

TYPO3: Enterprise Content Management

ISBN: 978-1-904811-41-1 Paperback: 624 pages

The Official TYPO3 Book, written and endorsed by the core TYPO3 Team

1. Easy-to-use introduction to TYPO3

2. Design and build content rich extranets and intranets

3. Learn how to manage content and administrate and extend TYPO3

Please check **www.PacktPub.com** for information on our titles

TYPO3 Extension Development

ISBN: 978-1-847192-12-7   Paperback: 232 pages

Developer's guide to creating feature rich extensions using the TYPO3 API

1. Covers the complete extension development process from planning and extension generation through development to writing documentation

2. Includes both front-end and back-end development

3. Describes TYPO3 areas not covered in the official documentation (such as using AJAX and eID)

4. Hands on style, lots of examples, and detailed walkthroughs

Joomla! 1.5 Multimedia

ISBN: 978-1-847197-70-2   Paperback: 357 pages

Build media-rich Joomla! web sites by learning to embed and display Multimedia content

1. Build a livelier Joomla! site by adding videos, audios, images and more to your web content

2. Install, configure, and use popular Multimedia Extensions

3. Make your web site collaborate with external resources such as Twitter, YouTube, Google, and Flickr with the help of Joomla! extensions

4. Follow a step-by-step tutorial to create a feature-packed media-rich Joomla! site

Please check **www.PacktPub.com** for information on our titles